D1480038

DEFINING AMERICAN INDIAN LITERATURE

DEFINING AMERICAN INDIAN LITERATURE
LITERATURE
One Nation Divisible

Robert L. Berner

Native American Studies
Volume 6

The Edwin Mellen Press
Lewiston•Queenston•Lampeter

Library of Congress Cataloging-in-Publication Data

Berner, Robert L., 1928-
  Defining American Indian literature : one nation divisible/
Robert L. Berner.
      p. cm. -- (Native American studies ; v. 6)
    Includes bibliographical references [and index].
    ISBN 0-7734-8039-0
    1. American literature--Indian authors--History and criticism. 2.
  Indians of North America--Intellectual life. 3. Indians in
  literature. I. Title. II. Series.
    PS153.I52 B47 1999
    810.9' 897--dc21
                                                              99-26137
                                                                  CIP

This is volume 6 in the continuing series
Native American Studies
Volume 6 ISBN 0-7734-8039-0
NAS Series ISBN 0-88946-482-0

A CIP catalog record for this book is available from the British Library.

Copyright © 1999 Robert L. Berner

All rights reserved. For information contact

        The Edwin Mellen Press   The Edwin Mellen Press
              Box 450   Box 67
        Lewiston, New York   Queenston, Ontario
        USA 14092-0450   CANADA L0S 1L0

                      The Edwin Mellen Press, Ltd.
                      Lampeter, Ceredigion, Wales
                      UNITED KINGDOM SA48 8LT

                  Printed in the United States of America

PS
153
.I52
B47
1999

081999-7995 K8

For Connie

-- for saving my life

TABLE OF CONTENTS

FOREWORD

This book originates in my belief that the study of the work of contemporary American Indian writers is complicated by problems in definition which critics, scholars, teachers, and editors so far have not addressed adequately.

The reader must understand at the outset that my subject is not traditional tribal mythology, folklore, and song but the use of tribal cultures by scholars and others, including Indians who have written in the last three or four decades of this century. I have sought to suggest solutions to the problems which I believe plague the systematic study of the work of those writers by posing and offering answers to questions which are so basic that many may wonder why I believe they must be asked:

1) What is an American Indian writer?

2) What are the legitimate literary uses of Indians and their culture?

3) Can an American Indian literary tradition be defined?

4) What is the relation of American Indian literature to America's literary tradition as a whole?

In the past twenty-five years as I have taught the subject, written about a number of contemporary Indian writers in a variety of articles and book reviews, and become increasingly perplexed, I have worked toward tentative answers to these questions which are the subject of the following essays.

This book is in no way intended to constitute a history of the literature of the American Indian. I apologize for ignoring writers some may consider essential to an understanding of the subject and for giving greater attention to others who might assume less importance in a balanced and comprehensive historical study.

But I do not apologize for what may seem to some an occasionally testy tone. The present state of American culture in my view is so dismal, indeed so foreboding, that rough measures are called for. I have meant to be provocative, though I hope that if I irritate readers it will be toward a realization that until my questions are addressed we must expect continued difficulty in pursuing a disciplined study of contemporary writing by Indians.

The "one nation divisible" to which the title refers is our country in its present predicament, a sad parody of those related ideals of the Pledge of Allegiance and the "melting pot" which have always been assumed to be the political and social basis of American unity, achieved through the wisdom of the Founding Fathers and maintained through the trials of civil war, economic catastrophe, and international conflict. The present crisis, I believe, is only the latest stage in the continuing American struggle to make a political system out of regional and economic diversity and a society and culture that can sustain it. The fashionable political ideal of our time -- fashionable among our intellectuals, that is -- is one of confrontation, of conflict between races, sexes, and classes, and of denial of anything like a cultural or social consensus or a common American consciousness. I believe that our intellectuals, at least those of them who actually care whether we survive as a nation, would be wise to give up their search for yet other ways to divide the American people and to concentrate their attention on a search for a common American identity -- not one which attempts to make white people out of people who aren't white but one which seeks to make Americans out of all the groups in our society. The essays which follow are my contribution to that search.

A final note: when I have referred to the descendants of the original inhabitants of the western hemisphere I always have chosen to call them American Indians. I understand the impulse behind the preference of many for the term *Native American*, and I know that Indian is the result of historical error. But for that matter so is *American*, which derived from a misreading of a reference to the first name of an Italian explorer on an early sixteenth century map. The truth of the matter is that our own country is not the only one in the world to receive its name by left-handed methods. The name of Brazil originates in mythology, France takes its name from a Germanic tribe, and Russia from the name of a tribe of Swedish Vikings.

I have never given much thought to Amerigo Vespucci when using the term

American. I have always assumed that an *American* is (1) a citizen of the United States of America or (2) an inhabitant of the western hemisphere, and *native*, as the dictionary's commonly accepted definition denotes, refers to birth. A "native American," therefore, is someone who is a citizen of the United States or an inhabitant of the western hemisphere because of birth. By that definition and by either of the above meanings of American I am a native American and the child of *native American* parents.

Of course, people who insist on everyone saying "Native American" are much more concerned with the promotion of their own political agenda than with anyone's concern for exact terminology. But I think it significant that the great majority of Indians, at least a majority of those I have met, call themselves Indians, particularly if they possess any thorough understanding of their tribal traditions, because they understand that the people Europeans encountered in America in the sixteenth century were members of hundreds of distinctive nations, each with its own language or dialect and its own culture and traditions. In fact, I have noticed that many Indians who insist on being called Native Americans lack any real understanding of tribal traditions that actually are derived from experience and very often are descended from at least some ancestors who, like all of mine, came to this continent from Europe.

To put it another way, we will be better off as Americans when we realize that what ails the condition of Indians -- and the condition of the rest of us as well -- has very little to do with nomenclature, easy as it is to blunder into that blind alley and think that it's the main street. The muddying of the linguistic waters by supposedly well-meaning people, including many non-Indians who are certain that they know what's best for their "Native Americans," is as grievous a condition in the study of American Indian cultures and American Indian writing as it is in the study of every other aspect of our woeful culture. Perhaps if we make an effort to get at what words really mean we may make a start in cleaning the messy house that the academic study of our culture has become.

PREFACE

For much of our history the national discourse about Indians has been a closed dialogue among popular fantasies about a people who are conveniently remote from the lives of the vast majority of Americans. Each age has thus been able to fantasize its own Indian: untameable savage, child of Nature, steward of the earth, the ultimate victim of modern civilization. At the same time, unmoored from the realities of modern Indian life, we have surrounded ourselves; with allusions to the Indian of our imagination, driving "Cherokees" and "Apaches" that automakers suggest will endow us with a rugged self-sufficiency lacking in our late twentieth century lives, devouring New Age tracts (mostly written by non-Indians) that claim to reveal esoteric native practices that supposedly will enable us to create some magical bond with the earth, attending Hollywood films that have replaced old stereotypes of the savage "Redskin" with new sanitized images of Indians as martyrs to the white man's greed.

Given our mythical way of thinking about Indians in general, it is perhaps predictable that we tend to see living Indians as so fundamentally unique that the books and other works of art produced by people who consider themselves to be Indian must defy normal criteria of analysis. In this provocative book, Robert L. Berner skillfully dismantles many of the pieties that continue to cloud our perceptions of "Indian" authors, a tricky term that like so much that has to do with Indians is not nearly as plain as it appears. While the framework for these essays is a rethinking of the ways in which we think and write about Indian literature, they also represent an ambitious attempt to place real-world Indians in a larger context of cultural assimilation: that is, a constant process of influence and counter-influence that has deeply affected Americans of all ethnic origins.

No tribal culture is what it was in 1492, Berner points out. (It is a telling measure of out confusion about who Indians really are today that such obvious truths need to be reiterated.) By the same token, however, Euro-Americans and other immigrants were deeply and irrevocably affected by their contact with Indians. American Indian literature is as inextricably entangled with the broader American culture as are the bloodlines of Indians with those of other Americans. While some Indian writers are solidly rooted in tribal background -- Berner cites Simon Ortiz and Lucy Tapahonso as examples -- many are Indian largely by self-definition, including some who, raised far from reservations and without tribal affiliation, can claim only vague or remote tribal lineage and others who, though raised in or near Indian Country, embody a fundamentally non-traditional literary sensibility. All write in English and many of them could easily claim to be white writers if they wished to. Berner's aim is not to categorize talented writers by their degrees of "Indianness," but rather, to recognize the complexity of Indian identity and, perhaps even more important, the intricate relationship of those writers with the non-Indian culture that has enabled them to become writers in the first place. He points out, for instance, that *The Way to Rainy Mountain,* by N, Scott Momaday, a man of mixed Kiowa, Cherokee and white ancestry, is the product not only of family tradition and tribal lore, but also of Momaday's distinctively personal sensibility, as well as his scholarly study of white anthropological writings on the Kiowa.

Berner argues that racial distinctions that we continue to apply to Indians as a matter of convention are at best anachronistic; at worst they have corrupted our critical judgment. He looks instead toward a common American identity that is roomy enough to include both Indians and Euro-Americans, as well as other minorities. "Every American, knowing it or not," Berner writes, "is a European *and* an Indian *and* an African living in the American landscape." By understanding both Indian writers and the larger literary culture of which they are a vital part, Berner believes that it is possible to better understand what he calls "the essential unity of the diverse elements of American experience." It hardly needs to be said that this challenges the fashionable idea that America is little more than a cultural background where a multitude of irreconcilable cultures endlessly contend, and the equally insidious notion that minority cultures must be walled off from the mainstream for their own protection.

Berner's courageous argument will permanently change the way we think about "Indian" literature.

Fergus M. Bordewich
Barrytown, NY

ACKNOWLEDGMENT

Though my thinking has since evolved, many of my ideas appeared first in the following articles and reviews, to the publishers and editors of which I am grateful:

"Charles L. McNichols and *Crazy Weather*: a Reconsideration." *Western American Literature* 6 (Spring 1971): 39-51.

"N. Scott Momaday: Beyond Rainy Mountain." *American Indian Culture and Research Journal* 3:1 (1979): 57-67.

Review: Peter G. Beidler. *Fig Tree John: An Indian in Fact and Fiction.* *American Indian Culture and Research Journal* 3:3 (1979): 84-87.

Review: *Zuni: Selected Writings of Frank Hamilton Cushing.* *American Indian Culture and Research Journal* 4:3 (1980): 100-104.

"Trying To Be Round: Three American Indian Novels." *World Literature Today* 58 (Summer 1984): 341-344.

Review: Lance Henson. *Selected Poems 1970-1983.* *American Indian Cultural and Research Journal* 11:3 (1987): 123-129.

"Lance Henson: Poet of the People." *World Literature Today* 64 (Summer 1990): 419-421.

"American Myth: Old, New, Yet Untold." *Genre* 25 (Winter 1992): 377-389.

"Columbus, Indians and American Literature." *World Literature Today* 66 (Spring 1992): 292-296.

Review: Lance Henson. *Another Distance: New and Selected Poems.* *World Literature Today* 66 (Summer 1992): 561.

Review: Gerald Vizenor. *Landfill Meditation.* *World Literature Today* 66 (Summer 1992]: 561-562.

"What Is An American Indian Writer?" in *Native American Values: Survival and Renewal*, ed. Thomas E. Schirer and Susan M. Branstner (Sault Ste. Marie: Lake Superior State University Press, 1993), pp. 124-135.

Review: Thomas King. *Green Grass, Running Water*. *World Literature Today* 67 (Autumn 1993): 869.

Review: Gerald Vizenor. *Manifest Manners: Postindian Warriors of Survivance*. *World Literature Today* 68 (Summer 1994): 616.

Review: Adrian C. Louis. *Vortex of Indian Fevers*. *American Indian Culture and Research Journal* 20 (1996): 259-263.

CHAPTER I

WHAT IS AN AMERICAN INDIAN WRITER?

Though editors seem to be in general agreement as to who American Indian writers are, any examination of what those writers say about themselves reveals such a wide range of background and experience, to say nothing of race, that we may suspect that editors tend to take the easy way of assuming that Indian writers are just writers who say they are Indians.

If we are to approach this subject honestly we must understand the implications of basic questions. Is the American Indian identity among writers a matter of race, or is it a matter of culture? Are they born with it, or do they acquire it? And if they acquire it, do they inherit it from their own experience of a tribal culture, or do they acquire it by study? And if it is the result of study, why is that process any different from anyone else's study of a tribal culture?

When we define a literary work in terms of its author's race we degrade not only the author but anyone who wishes to respond to the work in the light of its human and artistic value. It seems more appropriate, therefore, to say that an American Indian writer is not just somebody with Indian ancestors but one who has been reared in the culture of a particular tribe, feels that tribal identity in mind and emotions, and thinks in virtually every way as members of that tribe think.

Certainly tribal identity is the only one that American Indian tribes traditionally considered important. Indeed one of the most attractive features of traditional tribal life was the assumption of tribal members that their superiority was not racial but tribal. In fact, the historical record suggests that from the beginning and continuing through the nineteenth century tribes took no account of race at all. The many historical examples of tribal adoption suggest that, regardless of race, anyone under the right circumstances could become a member of a tribe. Consider, for example, the case of Cynthia Parker, who was found by Comanche raiders in the ruins of her parents' Texas ranch but in every way but racial inheritance was a Comanche because she was adopted by Comanche parents, thoroughly acculturated as a Comanche, and honored among her people as the mother of a great Comanche war chief. Tribal identity was not a matter of race.

But that was a long time ago. What we must wonder today is whether editors would consider Cynthia Parker an American Indian writer if she were alive and writing poetry or fiction out of her Comanche experience.

We may be tempted to doubt it when we consider the rather special case of Carter Revard, a Rhodes scholar who became a professor of medieval literature and who considers himself -- and is identified as -- an Osage poet. His mother separated from his father, who was "part Indian" (apparently Ponca), when Revard was a child and married a half-Osage man who spoke Osage and gave his own children and also his step-son a thorough understanding of Osage traditions. Revard, that is to say, is an Osage by adoption, and his Osage experience provides him with an American Indian angle of vision when he writes poems. In other words, he has inherited two identities -- not only thoroughly Osage by culture but Indian enough "by blood" -- to be labeled an American Indian writer.

But what if his natural father had not had that bit of Indian "blood"? What if Carter Revard in race had been only white and an Osage only by adoption, as Cynthia Parker was a Comanche only by adoption? Would there then be any place for him in anthologies of American Indian literature?

And what would be the difference between an all-white Carter Revard who would be thoroughly Osage because of adoption and a white writer who, through study and determination, made himself an Osage in culture? Consider, for example, the notorious case of Jamake Highwater, a Greek-American named Gregory J. Markopoulos who renamed himself, passed himself off as Blackfoot and/or Cherokee, studied various Indian cultures, received grants as an Indian because foundations believed that was what he was and found publication for a number of books which purport to define the special qualities of Indian culture and experience as only an Indian can know them (Kehoe 196). Certainly he must be credited with a considerable audacity. In a 1980 article -- which he had the gall to publish in an Indian publication -- he attacked what he called the "exclusivity and cultural snobbery" of tribal members who refused to accept individuals of Indian ancestry who possessed no tribal status (Hagan 320). Is his case only one of deception -- clearly it is that -- or, as we must suspect, just another example in our culture of a white person who wants to play Indian? (Adolf Gutohrlein, who named himself Adolf Hungry Wolf and made himself enough of a Blackfoot to be adopted by the Blood tribe in Alberta -- apparently they later cast him out -- is another example, though his pigmentation and German accent, had he wanted to deceive, are obvious [Kehoe 193-194].)

Brian Swann has defined Indians in a way that eliminates both Highwater and Hungry Wolf:

> Native Americans are Native Americans if they say they are, if other Native Americans say they are and accept them, and (possibly) if the values that are held close and acted upon are values upheld by the various native people who live in the Americas (Niatum xx).

Like all definitions of Indian identity this one poses problems. Only the first requirement is precise -- an Indian must claim to be an Indian. But to what extent must other Indians accept such a claimant? Does that mean tribal membership? Is that membership to be defined by tribal elders or by the vote of a majority of tribal members or by the Bureau of Indian Affairs or by Indian editors of anthologies -- or whom? And why the parenthetical *possibly* for adherence to Indian values? And, most complicating of all, to how many of the "various native people who live in the Americas" is Swann referring? Does he mean the whole hemisphere?

Swann's definition means, presumably, that "Highwater" was an Indian until he got caught and that "Hungry Wolf" never has been an Indian. But the latter case is more complex than that. "Hungry Wolf," to his credit, never claimed to be an Indian in race, but he certainly claimed to be one in culture, tribal awareness, and "spirit".

Perhaps the easiest way to deal with a white writer who wants to be an Indian badly enough to invent an Indian name and identity and even to lie about it to editors, grant reviewers, university officials, tribal elders, and a gullible public is to admit the legitimacy of Louise Erdrich's explanation of why she has identified with her Chippewa ancestors even though they are heavily out-weighed in her genes by Europeans and French Canadians. She has said in an interview that the Indian element in one's heritage is the strongest "because that is the part of you that is culturally different. When you live in the mainstream and you know that you're not ... really there, you listen for a voice to direct you" (Bruchac, *Survival* 77). She meant, presumably, that when a person aware of even a small degree of Indian "blood" and (presumably) tribal culture is immersed in a society and culture that are predominantly non-Indian even a slight Indian cultural heritage assumes an importance all out of proportion to its degree.

Actually this powerful sense of being Indian because the Indianness stands out against the surrounding whiteness is in social groups akin to the remarkable case of the Lumbees of North Carolina, whose case of deliberate tribe-making has been examined with apparent definitiveness by Karen Blu. The Lumbees have no records of treaties, no reservation, no Indian language, no customs that seem particularly "Indian," and no certain knowledge of their origins in any tribe (1). Their "tribal" name, in fact, was made up from that of the Lumber River, which flows through Robeson County, where most of them live. Hamilton McMillan, a local white historian, argued in 1888 that they had to be the descendants of the Raleigh colony which disappeared in the late sixteenth century after carving on a tree the word *Croatoan*, the name of a nearby island. Supposedly these English intermarried with nearby Indians, and their descendants drifted to Robeson County, where white settlers found them in the mid-eighteenth century. McMillan made up a name for them: *Croatan*. In 1894 John R. Swanton, a scholar of considerable resources, concluded that they were descendants of various Carolina Siouan tribes (Cheraw in particular). In 1913 a local politician decided that they were descended from escapees from the roundup of Cherokees who were sent to Indian Territory in the 1830's (40-41). The General Assembly of North Carolina recognized them legally as the "Croatan Indians" in 1885, as the "Indians of Robeson County" in 1911, as the "Cherokee Indians of Robeson County" in 1913, and finally in 1953 as the "Lumbee Indians" (236-237).

But the principal fact about the Lumbees, in population now one of the largest Indian groups in the country, is that they have maintained a powerful sense of themselves as Indians. Why? As we might expect, because of nothing but race. Their motives must be understood in part in the light of the case of the so-called "Jackson Whites" of the Ramapo Mountains of northern New Jersey, traditionally assumed to be the descendants of late eighteenth century freed blacks, runaway slaves, and Dutch farmers. Their campaign to gain status and federal acceptance as the "Rampough Indian Tribe" was based less on clear historical acceptance than on their denial of even partial descent from black slaves, understandable considering the prejudice they have encountered from those who have accepted the "Jackson White" legend (Mayer).

Robeson County, the homeland of the Lumbees, is about evenly divided between whites, African Americans, and Lumbees. The Lumbees do not claim to be white, and certainly in North Carolina they have not wanted to endure the discrimination that would result from being confused with African Americans. So they are Indians, though most Lumbees recite McMillan's Lost Colony yarn as historical fact and consider themselves descendants not only of the original Indians of the North Carolina coast but of Raleigh's English settlers, who, they are pleased to believe, were all Elizabethan aristocrats (Blu 35).

A survey of the racial background of writers whose work is published in anthologies of American Indian literature suggests that the literary establishment assumes with the Lumbees that race is the only real distinction between Indians and the rest of us and that having been brought up Indian by family, clan, and tribe, no matter how thoroughly, is no better than bringing yourself up Indian. In other words, if Carter Revard were all-white and called himself Osage only because of the teachings of his adoptive father, editors would consider him only another Jamake Highwater. As far as they are concerned, culture is not enough.

But the fact is that a survey of anthologized Indian writers reveals not only a wide range of tribal background -- and in many cases the lack of it -- but widely varying degrees of Indian "blood," sometimes as little as an eighth and in several cases too little for the writer to be anything but vague about the amount. As far as editors are concerned, even the smallest dab of Indian "blood" is enough. Writers are considered Indian if they have at least one Indian ancestor, even one who died several generations back.

And why not leave it at that? The truth is that the simplicity of this definition is well within American traditions. For centuries African Americans have been assumed to be those Americans with even the smallest amount of African ancestry -- defined literally as "one drop of blood." Even those white enough to "pass" would be labeled African American if they were found out. It's a preposterous definition, but we can deny neither its simplicity nor its clarity.

The problem with admitting into the canon of American Indian literature only those who are able to prove biological identity as Indians is that it denies the importance of the tribal tradition that gives an Indian culture its power and significance. When we examine what Indian writers say about themselves in autobiographical essays collected by Brian Swann and Arnold Krupat (1987) and what some of the same writers and others said in interviews with Joseph Bruchac (1987) and Laura Coltelli (1990), we find that the wide spectrum from extreme to extreme is in fact double. The most obvious reveals a range from those who are more less "pure" Indian in race -- with no European ancestors or at least none that are not too far back to count -- to those who if they wished could easily identify themselves as entirely white. But there is also a spectrum of writers ranging from those who in culture are rooted deeply in a tribal tradition to those who have no sense of a tribal tradition at all though they label themselves parenthetically according to a tribe, or to two tribes or even three. These two spectrums and their complex inter-relationship can be understood by considering the following representative figures:

(1) The gene pool of the Acoma tribe, like that of other pueblo tribes to one degree or another, no doubt includes Hispanic elements, but if Simon Ortiz has Spanish ancestors he takes no notice of them. He speaks the language of Acoma, and though he has been out in "the world" for his military service and education, he is fully a product of Acoma and able to identify fully with its cultural heritage. He often writes about Acoma subjects, and his people fully identify with him, on one occasion electing him lieutenant governor of the tribe.

(2) James Welch, who is of mixed Blackfoot and Gros Ventre descent, grew up close to, but not within, the traditions of both tribes. Apparently this gave him what he considers a creative balance of subjectivity and objectivity about the Blackfoot experience. "In some ways," he told Bruchac, "I was fortunate in growing up. I was not within the culture in some ways, but I was also not an outsider" (320). His historical novel *Fools Crow* (1986) is apparently a product of this balance, deriving in part from family tradition but also to a large degree from extensive research into Blackfoot history and ethnology.

(3) In *The Names* (1976) N. Scott Momaday acknowledges his mother's white and Cherokee ancestry, but he has concentrated his literary attention on his paternal Kiowa identity because of his experience in Kiowa country in Oklahoma as a child.

His Kiowa book, *The Way to Rainy Mountain* (1969), is a product of his memory of his grandmother's stories, but it also is based on his reading of white authors, in particular James Mooney's *Calendar History of the Kiowa Indians*. Furthermore, his childhood was largely spent in the pueblo of Jemez, and though he was an outsider there he knows its culture and traditions from personal experience, which is the primary source of his novel *House Made of Dawn* (1968).

(4) Wendy Rose grew up the victim not only of her mother's white relatives, who condemned her for her Indian "blood" but of an abusive Hopi father who once, in an alcoholic rage, attempted to strangle her. Because Hopi identity is understood in terms of matrilineal clans, she has "no real legitimate place in Hopi society," and "culturally I would have to say I'm ... an urban, Pan-Indian kind of person" (Coltelli 122-123). For that reason, apparently, she labels herself "Hopi-Miwok" because of an Indian seen in one of her mother's family pictures who she assumes to have been Miwok. But as a professional anthropologist she has spent a lot of time in Hopi country, studying Hopi culture and identifying with the tribe -- as she also has done with her mother's Scottish ancestors -- by an apparent act of will.

(5) Diane Glancy has been inspired by the example of a half-Cherokee grandmother who died when Glancy was thirteen. Geary Hobson has listed Glancy among poets who are "so tenuously tied by blood and upbringing to tribal cultures ... that they are hardly to be reckoned seriously among the more authentic Oklahoma Indian poets" ("Literature" 429), but in an autobiographical essay published in 1987 she said that "I am part heir to the Indian culture, and even that small part has leavened the whole lump," though in the same piece she also said, "I know little of my Indian heritage" and "I have the feeling of being split between the two cultures, not fully belonging to either one" (Swann and Krupat 169, 171). Since that interview, however, she seems to have become Cherokee through research, and *Pushing the Bear* (1996), her novel about the Cherokee "Trail of Tears," is a product of historical scholarship, her study of the Cherokee language and the syllabary of Sequoyah, and a powerful assertion of will.

(6) Jim Barnes, a professor of comparative literature who has translated German poetry and written a book about Thomas Mann, is one-eighth Choctaw and "proud of the Choctaw blood I carry" but identifies himself parenthetically as "Welsh-Choctaw" and objects to terms like "*ethnic writer* or even *Native American writer* though it may apply to a number of us in a general sense" (Swann and Krupat, 92, 94).

What are we to make of such a wide range of racial and cultural background? The most obvious fact about it is that except for claiming Indian ancestors these six writers, and others who could have been cited as easily, share little more than a powerful sense of being Indians. But do we really want to define an Indian writer as one who possesses -- or claims to possess -- a powerful sense of being Indian? Is becoming an Indian really only a matter of will? Is Jamake Highwater an Indian? Is Adolf Hungry Wolf?

In this connection it is worth mentioning the curious fact that the 1980 census reported a seventy-two percent increase in the Indian population of the United States over that of 1970 (Feraca 30) and that an additional increase of forty-five percent occurred between 1980 and 1990 (Statistical Abstract). Between 1960 and 1990, in fact, the American Indian population of the United States quadrupled. Obviously statistics for birth and death rates cannot explain this increase, and the fact is that the census only asked informants to check the box they preferred. For census purposes a Filipino or a Samoan or a Swede could turn himself into an Indian. One suspects, in other words, that for social and cultural reasons that we can only wonder about there are many Americans who at one time considered themselves white but have now decided to identify with an Indian ancestor, even one dead several generations back, or even one merely rumored in family legend, or even one for whom they can only wish. It is remarkable, in fact, that only seventy-four percent of those who identified themselves as Indians on the 1990 census returns also reported Indian ancestry (Wright 53).

The truth of the matter is that the census records probably do not begin to take adequate account of the extent to which the American population includes Indian ancestry in its gene pool. Given the fact that our population has been developing for almost four centuries, we probably should assume that ten or even twenty million Americans have "Indian blood." Consider, as a startling example, those who, by the loose definitions of the U.S. Census, could claim to be Indians because they are descendants of Pocahontas. Thomas Rolfe, the son of John and Rebecca (Pocahantas) Rolfe, grew up in England, returned to Virginia to claim his inheritance, and fathered Jane Rolfe, who married Robert Bolling and is the ancestor of an estimated two million Americans, including the "First Families" of Virginia -- Bolling, Randolph, Marshall, Lee, Lewis, Jefferson, and others (Young 177-178). In fact, her marriage to a white man makes her a symbolic figure in the evolution of a multiracial America, given the fact that an estimated seventy per cent of American Indians, a "race" which, as we have seen, includes not only the many with some European ancestry but the many other self-identified Indians who are primarily white in "blood," presently marry outside their "race" (Wright 49).

Perhaps the willingness of new "Indians" to check the appropriate box on their census forms is evidence that no stigma is any longer attached to being not quite white. Or perhaps -- and in the present cultural climate this seems more likely -- it is no longer chic to be white in general and Anglo-Saxon in particular.

But if we want to be honest with this phenomenon we will admit that the growth of the "Indian" population in this country must also be to some extent a consequence of the discovery of the economic advantages in becoming Indian, a discovery by no means made only in the last quarter of the twentieth century. For example, in the latter half of the nineteenth century the lands of the Five Civilized Tribes of Oklahoma (Cherokee, Choctaw, Chickasaw, Creek, and Seminole) were inundated with white squatters. By 1890 seventy percent of the population of Indian Territory were not Indians. A small percentage were the ex-slaves of tribesmen, but most were white men, some of whom had married Indian women but many others with no legitimate legal claims at all, who sought to get onto the tribal rolls so that they could get access to tribal land (Hagan 311). The Dawes Severalty Act also generated an enormous effort by non-Indians to convince themselves and others that they were Indians. These strategies continue in our own day as we see dubiously Indian opportunists seeking student aid reserved for Indians, access to federal assistance programs, and a slice of multimillion dollar judgments in land claims cases. As Hagan puts it, "Every announcement of a large judgment seemed to trigger the memories of some Americans that their family trees included an Indian, usually a chief's daughter, a princess" (318-319).

The fact is that the federal government and various tribes have collaborated in the creation of thin and often vague definitions of what constitutes tribal membership. For one example, persons with an Indian ancestor as far back as the eighth generation have been included in tribal land allotments (Berry 8), in other words, a great-great-great-great-great-great grandparent -- 1/256 Indian "blood" -- an ancestor born at least two hundred years ago. Whatever the motives of bureaucrats and tribal leaders, can the "Indians" who accepted land on these terms be innocent of fraud?

And that is by no means the worst of it. The case of the Pequots of Connecticut is only the most preposterous example of the efforts in recent years of a hundred groups to seek federal recognition as tribes for the sake of economic advantages. In 1974 the Pequot "tribe" was fifty-five people, actually a single family, on 212 acres of a state Indian reservation in Connecticut. Then they incorporated and went after state and federal money. These efforts, along with a court settlement that resulted from a suit against local landowners for property the Pequots lost in the nineteenth century, brought in by 1986 more than two and a half million dollars. Needless to say, all of this led finally to a casino. And also, needless to say, tribal membership has dramatically increased. In twelve years the original fifty-five Pequots were joined by almost three hundred other enterprisers who discovered, come to think of it, that they were Pequots, too (Hagan 324-325).

This suggests yet another point. The phenomenon of the "white shaman" --

those non-Indian poets who have been condemned by Indians for exploiting sacred materials which they can only know from their reading of ethnological reports and then laying claim to a knowledge of Indian spiritual experience as great as, or even greater than, that of any Indian -- suggests that Indianness, even if it is more or less purloined, can be an advantage in our culture. (This phenomenon will be examined more fully in the next chapter.)

So where are we? All we have found so far is a definition of an Indian writer as one who is at least slightly Indian in race and may or may not know anything about the culture and traditions of any tribe.

Can we define American Indian literature according to its themes? Do Indian writers deal with subjects and themes unavailable to other writers? Or if they are available, do Indian writers bring to them an awareness or insight or wisdom denied to the rest of us?

N. Scott Momaday, in his interview with Bruchac, indicated a number of attitudes and themes which he finds in the work of Indian writers more than elsewhere. The importance of the land and a sense of place within the natural environment are perhaps the most obvious. The Indians of the Southwest, he said, live not on the land but in it and are not alienated either from the land or from their people living in it. "The whole worldview of the Indian is predicated upon the principle of harmony in the universe" (*Survival* 180). In addition, he said, "the Indian has the advantage of a rich spiritual experience" and a sense of community and of tribal heritage, the sense, that is, of knowing one's relationship to one's ancestors. The sense of a relationship to an oral tradition is related to this, says Momaday, because singing and story-telling carry on traditional values and enhance a sense of relationship to a tribal tradition (*Survival* 186-187).

These assumptions are echoed by other Indian writers and are accepted as characteristically Indian by non-Indians who write about the subject. But given the testimony of some who are included in the apparent corpus of American Indian literature that they have little or no experience with a tribal culture and know it only through study, are the themes and attitudes indicated by Momaday the inevitable consequence of being an Indian? Or, conversely, are those themes and attitudes impossible in a non-Indian?

The fact of the matter is that Momaday himself seems unable to get this problem straight in his mind. Arnold Krupat has quoted his references (in a piece published in 1987) to "the memory in my blood" and to "intrinsic variables in man's perception of his universe that are determined to some extent on the basis of his genetic constitution" (13). This baloney, no matter how you slice it, assumes a racial premise. And yet in the Bruchac interview (also published in 1987) Momaday suggested that non-Indian writers also may be capable of the rich spiritual experience which is one of the attributes which he identifies as Indian. And when we consider the other attitudes he mentions -- a sense of universal harmony, of community, of relationship to an oral tradition -- we surely must doubt that they are limited to Indian writers. Of course, a white writer who possessed a sense of community could hardly claim to derive it from a tribal heritage. But what is that to the purpose? The truth is that writers who call themselves Indians though they lack tribal experience have the same difficulty. Momaday defines this sense of community in terms of knowing one's relationship to one's ancestors, and he cites his white students, who often tell him that they wish they knew something about their ancestors. But a real understanding of what white grown-ups know and think and believe is hardly to be found by asking young people, and the explosion of genealogical research in America in recent years, hardly the work of the young, suggests not only that appreciation of one's ancestors requires maturity but that this sense is less Indian than American in general. In fact, Momaday himself, if his family history *The Names* is evidence, has really discovered a large part, if not most, of what he knows about his ancestors as historical beings the way the rest of us have discovered ours -- by research in libraries and public records.

We would do better in our quest for a definition of the American Indian writer by considering the implications of a remark by Wendy Rose, which though it begs the question and may be inexact in its key word, is useful: "There is no *genre* of 'Indian literature' .... There is only literature written by people who are Indian ...." This is echoed in Duane Niatum's simple assertion that there is no "Indian aesthetic that is different from a non-Indian" (both quoted in Niatum, p. xviii).

In other words, both Rose and Niatum seem to suggest the sensible proposition that poems are poems and fictions are fictions, that some are written by Indians and some are not, and that all must be judged according to literary rather than racial or ethnic or political standards.

In his better moments Momaday recognizes this same wisdom. In his Bruchac interview he admitted that the traditional Indian sense of what he calls "the magic of words" is found in an older European culture. "The Anglo-Saxon who uttered spells over his fields so that the seeds would come out of the ground by the sheer strength of his voice ... believed absolutely in the efficacy of language" (Bruchac, *Survival* 183). In other words, the difference between a European and an American Indian is a difference not in nation or culture and certainly not in race but in time: the traditional American Indian is what the European peasant once was.

Joy Harjo made the same point to Bruchac: "All people are originally tribal .... If European people look into their own history, their own people were tribal societies to begin with and they got away from it. That's called 'civilization'" (*Survival* 92). The difference, in other words, between Americans whose ancestors are Indian and Americans whose ancestors came from Europe is that because of a great passage of time the latter cannot be fully conscious of the tribal sources of community, family, and social and cultural heritage, which for an American Indian -- at least an Indian with tribal awareness -- are easier to understand because they are still present in the tribe.

Even though the inevitable implication of this is that anyone whose Indian identity is only racial is in the same boat with those of us whose ancestors came from Europe, this notion may seem to bring us somewhat nearer to a more meaningful definition than we have found so far: an Indian writer is one who is able to relate to traditional tribal concerns for language, community, ancestry, and the natural world because those concerns are still vital and organic in many tribes.

Still, we must remember where we began. The writers we have mentioned are not uniformly conscious of their tribal origins. Some, to one degree or another, derive from tribes, but others are urban, "pan-Indian" with sometimes wildly divergent identities (Sioux-Laguna, for example), and are simultaneously alienated from their European origins and unable to identify fully with a tribe. In other words, if Americans of European descent are cut off from their tribal origins, many, if not most, of those who consider themselves Indians are cut off from theirs. For most Indians, as for most of the rest of us in America, the recovery of a tribal sense is an act of will.

The truth of the matter is that analogies with the circumstances of European immigrants illuminate the plight of those Indian writers who, at least to a degree, are cut off from tribal traditions and thus determined to recover them as an exercise in self-definition. In fact, a statement made in 1916 by Randolph Bourne makes clear that resistance to the "melting pot" always has been an abiding feature of American society. As European immigrants established themselves and prospered they cultivated the cultural traditions of their homelands.

> Assimilation, ... instead of washing out the memories of Europe, made them more and more intensely real. Just as these clusters became more and more objectively American, did they become more and more German or Scandinavian or Bohemian or Polish (86).

In other words, the impulse to become American while retaining a cultural identity that is not American need not deny each other. In fact, as Bourne made clear, they enhance each other. Himself "Anglo-Saxon" in race, he looked forward to a "cosmopolitan" America, deriving its strength from more than its English traditions: "We [Anglo-Saxons] have needed the new peoples ... to save us from our own stagnation" (87). Of course, Bourne was referring only to "new peoples" from Europe, but his point is not invalidated by applying his generalization not only to present-day European immigrants but to immigrants from other parts of the world and to non-European Americans already here.

An interesting aspect of this problem is suggested by what we know of writing by Alaska "Natives." Bruchac has selected a representative body of it in one of his anthologies, *Raven Tells Stories* (1991). About a third of the twenty-three writers in this anthology are Eskimos, about a fourth are Tlingits, two are Aleuts, and most of the rest are from various Athabascan groups. Taken together, what we see in these writers is a higher percentage who derive directly from a traditional tribal culture than we usually find in anthologies of American Indian writing. The Eskimo writers in particular reveal a confidence in their relation to their traditional Eskimo culture, and this may explain the apparent ease with which they seem able to adapt into their traditional vision elements from the common American culture, even snowmobiles, television, and country-western music. They remain at peace with what is outside their tradition because they are so thoroughly Eskimo. They are, to borrow a useful term which Robert H. Davis, one of the Tlingit poets, applies to himself, "Neo-traditional" -- firmly rooted in tradition but open to non-traditional experience.

What this implies is that a writer who is most tribally aware will have the least difficulty coming to terms with other cultures, including the dominant culture that surrounds his own, while the writer who is less tribally aware will experience the greatest difficulty relating not only to a tribal tradition but to the dominant culture as well. On the other hand, what it also implies is that if a writer is able to reconcile a tribal culture to the culture outside the tribe the results may be of great value not only for other members of the tribe but for all of us. The fact is that not only is Joy Harjo right about all of us descending from tribes somewhere in the past but that all of us are in a sense tribal whatever our race and upbringing -- that is to say that we see our world from the angle of vision which we inherit as products of our culture and society. All of us are born into a social class, a society, a clan and family, and we are who we are because of that inheritance, which gives us strengths but which also flaws our vision when we consider those who have been born into other classes, societies, clans and families. And we are even more isolated than that because we all grow up to be individuals and thus separate from each other. The problem faced by American Indian writers, who all, to one degree or another, have had to deal with the problems inherent in the relationship of their tribe, or at least their race, to those outside it, is in fact a type of the problem we all face, and the way those writers deal with that isolation and find ways to escape it provides lessons for all of us.

As for the question with which we began -- just how are we to identify an American Indian writer as an American Indian writer -- we will be left with the definition with which we began unless we can find something better. I suggest a better in the proposition that Indian writers, unlike any others, seem most Indian when they seem most tribal and define the reality with which they deal in the light of tribal experience. I say tribal experience, not racial experience, not something that one claims to exist "in the blood" as part of a genetic inheritance, but a culture experienced and absorbed from the teaching of parents and elders, or at least observed at close hand, but in any case embraced in the heart. Of the six representative figures described above, Simon Ortiz definitely is an American Indian writer because of his Acoma experience; James Welch is a Blackfoot writer because he was, in his words, "within the culture in some ways" but also because he has fully studied Blackfoot reality; N. Scott Momaday is a Kiowa writer because of his experience in Kiowa country as a child and his study of Kiowa culture as an adult; Wendy Rose, whatever Hopi traditionalists may think, is a Hopi writer because as a poet she has embraced the Hopi reality she has studied and experienced as an anthropologist; and Diane Glancy was not a Cherokee writer in 1987 when she said she knew little of what she then called "my Indian heritage," but she is one now that she has discovered what it really is to be a Cherokee. The only one of the six who (apparently) is not an Indian writer is Jim Barnes, judging from what he himself has said about his Choctaw inheritance, which is for him a reason for pride but finally (again apparently) only a label.

The usefulness of this definition is that it escapes the limitations that are inevitable in any definition that proceeds from racial premises. In my view any definition of anyone solely in the light of racial origin diminishes the humanity of that person. On the other hand, it is possible to be both fully tribal and fully human, and our national history is rich with examples of individuals who were both -- Chief Seattle, Chief Joseph, Nicholas Black Elk, and Ishi, to name only four of many. Indeed the most valuable lesson we learn from the study of the lives of these four, who are not only great figures in the history of the Salish, Nez Perce, Lakota and Yahi people but great American historical figures as well, is that it is possible to be both fully tribal and fully human.

If we are not to be forever at each other's throats in America this is a lesson all of us must learn.

CHAPTER II

THE DOWNWARD PATH FROM CUSHING TO ROTHENBERG

In 1879, when the Bureau of American Ethnology mounted its first expedition to the western New Mexico pueblo of Zuni, its members included two remarkable individuals who can be considered representative figures in our understanding of the worst and the best in the way outsiders have dealt with the culture of tribal Indians. One of them, Matilda Coxe Stevenson, whose husband led the expedition, was a formidable and in many ways representative figure in what might be called the heroic age of American ethnology. She went to Zuni to amass artifacts and data, and her methods were, to say the least, direct. If she had to, she bought the artifacts from Zunis who probably would have preserved the materials of their tribal culture if they had been able to resist the money she offered. But on more than one occasion she barged into kivas to observe and photograph ceremonies, and when the Zunis objected she threatened to call in the militia -- perhaps not a bluff. She was neither the first nor the last social scientist to regard an Indian tribe as a resource to be exploited.

Gerald Vizenor's condemnation of anthropologists may seem extreme -- "Dead failures. They've never been right once" (Coltelli 169) -- but it is fairly typical of the almost universal loathing of anthropologists that is fashionable among American Indian writers, a loathing that originates in tribal memories of bad experiences with people like Matilda Stevenson, who was at best a snoop and at worst a corrupter of morals and even a pirate. But in the latter half of this century, when many Americans who are not Indian have pretended they are, Stevenson, whatever the value of the anthropological study of Indian tribes, must be considered the symbolic great-grandmother of those white poets who have exploited Indian sacred materials found in ethnological reports by claiming for themselves a superior knowledge of Indian spiritual experience. Wendy Rose, in an interview with Joseph Bruchac, made clear that she does not mind non-Indians writing about Indians. But "there are those who come out and say that they are Indians when they are not .... There are those [who] claim that what they write is somehow more Indian, or more legitimately Indian, than what real Indian people are writing" (*Survival* 267). The pose of the writers Rose condemns inevitably seems preposterous to the Indians in any audience to which they read their work.

Geary Hobson, apparently the first to call these poets "white shamans," understood their racket as just a new version of cultural imperialism. He cites such "well-meaning hot-shots" of the 1920's as Elsie Clews Parsons, Mabel Dodge, and D.H. Lawrence as earlier versions of the phenomenon ("Rise" 101). Considering these three figures peas in a pod because each of them was drawn to the pueblo of Taos seems somewhat wrong-headed. If Matilda Stevenson represents the bad side of the first generation of American ethnologists, Parsons was a better side of the generation that followed. Mabel Dodge Luhan at worst was guilty only of an embarrassing struggle to "go Indian," but she remains a pitiful figure because the Indian husband who was part of her assumed Indian identity gave her syphilis -- the last laugh, if that's what it was. As for Lawrence, he was really only a tourist and no more an exploiter than other tourists who are welcomed today as the guests of pueblos during ceremonial dancing. He was not a snooper into kivas, not a raider of artifacts, but a creative writer with a sincere appreciation of those qualities of ceremonial life at Taos which he believed were an implied criticism of what he considered the ills of Western civilization. In fact, much of what he said about

European civilization and about the pueblo vision as an alternative to it resembles what the present generation of American Indian writers say about Europeans and Indians. Indeed, one might suggest that the pervasive presence of Lawrence in the Taos area even years later has influenced the way many writers, white and Indian, have understood the ceremonialism of the Rio Grande pueblos and that Lawrence actually has influenced the way young Indian graduates of English programs in Southwest universities have seen that ceremonialism as an implied condemnation of what they choose to call "Anglo" culture.

But Hobson's basic point is correct. The "white shamans" can be categorized, as he categorizes them, with the hunters who began the destruction of the traditional cultures of the Plains by slaughtering the buffalo, with those who undermine a traditional Southwest reservation home industry by mass-producing "Indian jewelry," and with those "imperious anthropologists" who have cared more for their data and their dissertations than for the integrity of the cultures they have studied ("Rise"101).

> Writing from what they generally assume to be an Indian point of view ... and pontificating about their roles as remakers of the world through the power of their words, they seem to have no particular qualms about appropriating ... American Indian songs and poetry and then passing off their own poems based on those transliterations as the pronouncements of "shamans" ("Rise"101-102).

The poets he condemns are for the most part of little importance -- just who are Gene Fowler and Jim Cody? -- but Gary Snyder, though equally guilty as far as I can tell, is apparently too "significant" a figure for Hobson really to take to task: "The poems [of Snyder] contain great vitality and are, I believe, sincere efforts ..." ("Rise" 105). This timidity in attacking Snyder suggests that Hobson may have discovered more than he realizes: if Snyder is a good poet and Fowler and Cody aren't, then maybe what Hobson really means is that Indian materials *can* be used by non-Indian writers to make poems which not only can stand as works of art but can enhance the value of their Indian sources. Perhaps the only legitimate complaint to be made against those "white shamans" Hobson is willing to condemn can be stated more simply.

They just can't write.

But the most telling point Hobson makes about the "white shamans" is that their pose "not only cheapens the cultures which these true believers seek to join, but cheapens as well the culture from which they are fleeing." They must "restore themselves to their own houses -- by learning and accepting their own history and culture .... I am hoping that we can all learn to accept our histories -- and our ancestors -- for what they are and were" ("Rise" 107).

This criticism has been made by other American Indian writers. Leslie Marmon Silko, for example, has been quite willing to take Gary Snyder to task for failing in *Turtle Island* to acknowledge and come to terms with his own European roots. Until he -- and for that matter the rest of us -- do so, she says, "the 'rediscovery' which so many Americans are waiting for ... will be just another dead-end in more than two hundred years of searching for a genuine American identity" ("Old-Time" 199). Linda Hogan makes the same point, referring to the "shamans" as "non-Indians who are in spiritual crises [and] hope to gain from the ways of other cultures because they do not find their own ways to be valuable" (Swann and Krupat 244). Hogan realizes that in fact "most Indian people are living the crisis of American life ..." and that it is no easier for an Indian to be a shaman than it is for a non-Indian (Coltelli 75). Peter Blue Cloud condemns non-Indian poets for "concentrating on being 'very Indian' .... Why aren't they writing about themselves and what the hell do they know about Chief Joseph or Sitting Bull?" (Bruchac, *Survival* 31). Needless to say, Blue Cloud himself can achieve no understanding of Chief Joseph and Sitting Bull that white writers cannot achieve. Neither he nor they can discover those chiefs except in books. After all, if "Indian blood" -- Blue Cloud's only possible connection to Chief Joseph and Sitting Bull -- were all anyone needed to write worthwhile poems about such subjects, all Indians -- two million of them if the 1990 census returns are to be believed -- would be poets. Still, his basic complaint is to the point. The "shamans" have fastened themselves as parasites on tribal cultures because they cannot relate to their own origins. As he says, "Why aren't they writing about themselves?" Because, we must assume, they know very little about themselves and actually believe that they themselves are not really worth writing about. Perhaps they are right.

We can only wonder what these American Indian critics of the "white shaman" phenomenon would say about Frank Hamilton Cushing (1857-1900), the other member of the Stevenson expedition who is a representative figure for our understanding of the problems we have posed. Cushing certainly "went Indian." Only twenty-two years old when he arrived at Zuni, he was invited to live in the home of the pueblo's governor. He quickly began to learn the Zuni language and soon was participating in the activities of the pueblo and wearing Zuni clothing -- to the disgust of Matilda Stevenson, who considered him "the biggest fool and charlatan I ever knew" (*Zuni*, p. 24n). Photographs of Cushing in his Zuni togs make it easy to see why he disgusted so many of his Smithsonian colleagues and may tempt us to agree with their judgment of him as a poseur. But Matilda Stevenson was wrong. Cushing was not really a charlatan and he certainly was not a fool. He was what he said he was -- a student of Zuni culture who was able to get into the real life of Zuni not by forced entry but by submerging himself in the life of the pueblo and its people. If he had not been so young and so open to experience, his stay at Zuni almost certainly would have been something else. But the Zunis could see that he was a tabula rasa on which they could imprint their own vision and that Cushing, a truly humane man with a sense of the universal condition of humanity, would accept that vision without prejudice.

How he did this remains perhaps the most remarkable episode in American scholarship. When the rest of the expedition moved on, they abandoned him without a word and without supplies. He just got up one morning to find them gone. In this desperate situation the governor changed his life forever: "Now, if you do as we tell you, and will only make up your mind to be a Zuni, you shall be rich, for you shall have fathers and mothers, brothers and sisters, and the best food in the world" (*Zuni* 68).

In the next four and a half years Cushing achieved fluency in the Zuni language, was formally initiated into the tribe, and eventually became not only a Bow Priest but, incredibly, a member of the tribal council. In 1882 he accompanied a group of Zunis on a trip east, where his flair for the theatrical produced favorable publicity for his friends and the good opinion of certain journalists who were fascinated by him and later helped him expose a land-steal on the Zuni reservation. For his part in this episode Cushing received the undying affection of the Zunis and the enmity of powerful figures in Washington, one of them Senator John Logan of Illinois, who happened to be the father-in-law of one of the land thieves. Logan began what only can be called a personal vendetta, which produced a crisis for Cushing's friends in the Bureau of American Ethnology, who recalled him in the face of an apparent threat by Logan to destroy the Bureau if they did not. Fifty years later the older people at Zuni still remembered him with affection, and an anthropologist visiting there in 1938 frequently was told by one old man that if "Cushy" said it in his writings it was so (*Zuni* 21).

Cushing's achievements, given his short life, are astounding. His investigations at Zuni led him to the now accepted assumption that the original Zuni villages were Coronado's Seven Cities of Cibola, and when as leader of the Hemenway Expedition of 1886 he conducted "digs" in the Salado and Gila valleys he discovered the culture which later came to be called Hohokam. His writings on Zuni are not only pioneering works, but works of literature. *Zuni Breadstuff* (1884-1885), ostensibly a study of Zuni agriculture and food preparation, is actually a full account of the significance of corn in Zuni life and thus a full exposition of the tribal culture. His "Outlines of Zuni Creation Myths" (1896) formulated a seven-fold structure of classification based on the four directions, the zenith, the nadir, and the center which Cushing found to be fundamental in Zuni building design, agricultural methods, ritual observances, clan structures, burial practices, and indeed the whole of Zuni life. His posthumous *Zuni Folk Tales* (1901), though flawed by an old-fashioned "literary" language, remains valuable for comparison with later collections of Zuni myths and legends by Dennis Tedlock and others. And *My Adventures in Zuni* (1882-1883), a neglected minor masterpieces of American literature, is an astonishing account not only of the rhythms of Zuni life but of the process by which Cushing, as he came to understand those rhythms, achieved at the same time a self-knowledge and indeed a wisdom amazing in a man then only in his mid-twenties.

Cushing's insights were unappreciated by many of his critics during his life-time and could not be appreciated adequately by later scholars until more recent assumptions became commonplace -- structuralism, for example, and Whorf's conception of the inter-relation of language and world-view. As early as 1882 Cushing observed that the "remarkable archaic language" of the Zunis reveals evidence "of the primitive history, especially of the intellectual development of the people by whom it is spoken" (*Zuni* 107). His analysis of Zuni creation myths led him to assert that such studies "bear on the history of man the world over ..., for the Zunis ... are representative ... of a phase of culture through which all desert peoples, in the Old World as well as in the New, must sometime have passed " (*Zuni* 218). And Claude Levi-Strauss has credited Cushing with directly affecting the development of structuralism by influencing Durkheim and Mauss in their study of social structures. Indeed Cushing may be considered a pioneer of structuralist theory.

Of course, he made mistakes -- he was, for example, unaware of Spanish adhesions in Zuni culture -- but his experience with the Zunis demonstrates his passionate determination to deal with his subjects as real people in meaningful situations, and this passion suggests the difference between his procedures and those of his more "scientific" contemporaries. In 1895 he defended his "personal style" by asserting that "well-nigh all anthropology is personal history ...." The student of the artifacts of "past man," therefore, must become in imagination the original artisan of those artifacts.

> I have virtually the same hands he had, the same physique, ... the same actival and mental faculties, that men had in ages gone by, no matter how remote. If, then, I dominate myself with their needs, surround myself with their material conditions, aim to do as they did, the chances are that I shall restore their acts and their arts ..." (*Zuni* 17).

In other words, Cushing knew almost a century ago what has since become obvious -- that if, as physics since Einstein has made clear, the observer of an experiment is part of the experiment, then it is unlikely that the social sciences, given their human subject matter, can be completely scientific.

Whatever his limitations and however we might smile at photographs of Cushing in his Zuni regalia, he was not just "playing Indian." He was neither a "white shaman" nor a miner of artifacts. (If he had been, why would the Zunis have adopted him and remembered him with the greatest affection?) His Zuni experience offers a valuable lesson which few understood in his lifetime and which contemporary Indian intellectuals may, for ideological reasons, be unable or even unwilling to appreciate. That experience, after all, derived from his willingness to accept on its own terms an Indian culture, no matter how strange to "civilized" society and no matter how unrelated to Christian preconceptions. At a time when the assumptions of many otherwise humane people were flawed by racial stereotyping, religious bias, and cultural chauvinism, Cushing was able to accept and even embrace Zuni paganism and to insist to his readers that it was as valid and valuable a world-view as any of the world's religions, even Christianity. In fact, late in life (1897), in a speech to the Indian Commissioners, he insisted that only catastrophe could result from any attempt to wrench Indian people away from their traditional religious and cultural allegiances. This wisdom, shared unfortunately by too few of his contemporaries, even by too few friends of Indians, was the product of his happy life at Zuni, which he summed up in an 1880 letter as "a feast, a peace of mind unapproached in all my previous experience" (*Zuni* 145).

Cushing's writings succeed both as literature and as ethnology. Their human content and his wisdom in dealing with it far outweigh his errors as a scientist. But his contemporaries condemned him as a poseur and a charlatan, though what they really were complaining about was what they considered his lack of scientific objectivity, and later professional anthropologists have condemned him on those grounds. They assume that because he entered into the life of the people he studied he could not bring a scientist's detachment to the culture he observed. Franz Boas, for example, claimed that Cushing's failure to take account of Spanish elements in Zuni culture proved that his "psychological explanation," as Boas called it, was "entirely misleading" (317).

In other words, Cushing's writings about Zuni may fall between two stools of criticism -- not scientific enough to satisfy anthropologists and too scientific to escape Vizenor's general dismissal of all anthropologists as "dead failures."

As far as I'm concerned, the best defense of Cushing is an objective and thorough reading of what he wrote. That reading will discover nothing to suggest that he was unwilling to let the culture of Zuni speak for itself, no evidence that he manipulated his subject to conform to his own preconceptions, no patronization of the Zuni people. Of course, he looked at Zuni through his own eyes. How could he have used anyone else's? But to the extent that it was possible -- and no non-Zuni until now has surpassed him in this, and almost certainly none in the future will -- he saw the Zuni world from inside. What after all is the real complaint of Indians against anthropologists? For one thing, those with any awareness of the life actually lived on their home reservations resent being told that their tribal cultures are dying. Knowing that life, they know that the culture is alive and evolving like any other healthy organism. But they also resent the fact that anthropologists are objective and thus give the impression that they don't really give a damn about the people they examine with such great "objectivity." No "pose" adopted by Cushing was as terrible or unfeeling as this. He proceeded from a basic principle that must never be forgotten when we examine the life of Indians or anyone else -- that the people with whom he dealt were human beings before they were Zunis.

The moral of the story of Frank Hamilton Cushing and the Zunis would appear to be that ideally anthropologists and translators of tribal texts do the greatest justice to their subject when they let the people and the texts speak for themselves. Too often their efforts are marred by their preconceptions. Cushing's greatest virtue was his absolute acceptance of what he saw at Zuni with only one determination -- to discover what made it so characteristically a phenomenon of the life of the Zunis by understanding it in the light of their humanity, which he knew was essentially no different from his own. The truth about his "going Indian" is that he did not really become a Zuni at all. (Perhaps if he had he would have resigned from the Bureau when he was ordered back to Washington and remained in Zuni for the rest of his life.) In maintaining his humanity he respected the humanity of his Zuni friends. It was for himself, his human self, that the Zunis gave him their lasting affection.

The ideal Cushing represents is too often forgotten by some editors who have regarded the American Indian as an example of this, that, or the other and have structured their anthologies in that light. Several examples might be cited -- in a rising order of faults.

First there is the elementary mistake of defining the limits of the subject too carelessly, either including too much or too little. Andrea Lerner, for example, has assembled an anthology of what she considers "Northwest Native American writing." It might seem an impressive book were it not for one serious flaw. The writers she has selected are all associated in one way or another with the "Northwest," which she defines as such a huge slice of the North American continent that one can only wonder not why she included what she did but why she left out the rest. It's an enormous triangle, the points of which are eastern Montana, northern California and Nevada, and the Aleutian Islands -- all of Alaska, that is, all of Montana, and the three states which are usually considered the Pacific Northwest, plus a large chunk of California and Nevada. Leaving aside the question of whether anyone else has ever thought of the Northwest in such broad terms, one must wonder at her editorial principles in choosing her thirty-five writers. The fact is that, even using her broad definition of the Northwest, four of the twenty-nine writers whose birthplaces are indicated in introductory notes are not natives of that area, broad as it is, and eight of the thirty-two whose tribal affiliations are indicated do not derive from the area's tribes. Her apparent editorial principle was to pick writers who in one way or another share an interest in what she calls the "Northwest," no matter where they now live, *and* present residents of the area no matter what their tribal origins, *and* in one case, Jim Barnes, who usually is identified as "Choctaw-Welsh," a writer who can be identified with the area only because he once worked in Oregon as a lumberjack.

Another editor, Jerry D. Blanche, has assembled a *Native American Reader* which has the virtue of including examples of material that has appeared in publications of limited circulation by writers so far known only to small local audiences. Most of the publications in which the book's stories, poems, and speeches first appeared are obscure and hard to find, and that's a good thing. But in spite of its title and in spite of its full one hundred selections, it is in no sense representative of the full range of Native American writing. And this is not a matter of space limitation. Of the thirty-five poets, eleven are Choctaws, and though almost all of the speeches date from 1973 to 1989 Blanche has thrown in Pushmataha's famous 1812 reply to Tecumseh, apparently because it was too important a Choctaw text to leave out. This concentration on Choctaw writers, in fact, makes one wonder why *Choctaw* is not part of the title -- and also suspect that it may have something to do with Blanche's identification of himself as a Choctaw.

But Lerner and Blanche are commendable when compared to those editors who use the materials they select to justify their own ideological agenda. Consider, for example, Paula Gunn Allen's collection of several traditional stories and seventeen short stories by those "granddaughters" of "Spider Grandmother" whom she calls "warrior women." Allen is not above a certain amount of hocus-pocus to "prove" her claim that Indian women are most remarkable in their role as warriors. For example, she says that one story is about "a young girl's induction into a Pueblo tradition ... of war captain" and then almost in the same breath admits that as a matter of fact there *was* no such tradition (67).

Actually the stories, though very uneven in quality, an inevitable consequence of choosing them according to political rather than artistic criteria, are by no means what is most wrong with the anthology. Its sorriest aspect is Allen's lamentable introduction and notes, which seem to have been written only for those who read to reinforce their prejudices. For one thing, they are marred by incredible historical errors, some perhaps due to sloppy editing -- misspelling names, for example, and implying that Calhoun was Jefferson's secretary of state -- but by others which can only be the result of Allen's grasp of historical detail, which is, to put it most charitably, uncertain. These blunders might be considered slight imperfections if their pattern did not include others which inform her particular animus. For example, to prove her claim that "the Anglo-Americans who came here had one goal: destruction of life," she cites as "evidence" a manufactured "statistic" that in the twenty-five years after the Civil War these "Anglo-Americans" slaughtered "millions" of Indians in the West and then claims in a later reference to this slaughter that "No holocaust in this millennium has been more destructive" (12, 21). The reference to "Anglo-Americans" is significant. All of Allen's villains were not English or even British in nationality so by calling them "Anglo-Americans" she apparently means to define them by their common language. One would have thought that at least since the demise of Adolf Hitler the equation of race and language was discredited enough to be rejected by any educated person. But in tossing around the word *holocaust* she makes it clear that her anthology is not intended for anyone who knows what Hitler did to the Jews -- or for that matter what Pol Pot did to the people of Cambodia or Idi Amin to those of Uganda. Nor is it intended for anyone who knows anything at all about the nineteenth-century demography of the Great Plains, where most of the fighting between Indians and her "Anglo-Americans" took place. Indeed one wonders what any non-Indian or any man of any race or for that matter any Indian woman not loaded down with Allen's ideological baggage would make of her wild claims or of her apparent inability to say anything at all about the texts she has selected that is not merely and tiresomely political. The thrust of her argument proceeds from her wild genocidal charge -- which actually trivializes the real victims of events like those at Sand Creek and Wounded Knee by submerging them in her fictitious "millions" -- to a premise that American Indian women are "women at war" and then to a selection of texts which reveal women who are warriors or whose exploits Allen can interpret as warrior-like. One traditional story, says Allen, is about resistance to a "a white man from the East"; the narrator of another story says proudly, "I like to challenge men"; a story of "another warrior woman," says Allen, is a profound cry against "male domination"; and so on.

In other words, her enterprise collapses under the weight of her feminism, and because she has chosen to define the enemy of American Indian women as both male and white, her politics is that of the reverse sexism and reverse racism of the fashionably "progressive."

But the distortions of Lerner and Blanche and the pomposity and hysterical pontification of Allen fade before the outrageous posturing of Jerome Rothenberg. In 1972 he produced *Shaking the Pumpkin: Traditional Poetry of the Indian North Americans*, an anthology which received great acclaim as a breakthrough in the translation of traditional Indian song. For example, the title of an article by H.S. McAllister -- "'The Language of Shamans': Jerome Rothenberg's Contribution to American Indian Literature" -- implied a total acceptance of Rothenberg's program and his claim to special insight into the "shaman." Denying that Rothenberg's "cavalier disinterest in footnotes" did harm to appreciation of his texts and admitting that such appreciation "would be augmented by the provision of a cultural context," McAllister then laid out a defense of Rothenberg's procedures which was clearly derived from his belief that Rothenberg was correct "in his perception of the analogy between traditional Indian poetry and the Beat, Projective and Concrete movements ..." (294, 309).

But defenders of Rothenberg ought to have taken account of what William

Bevis said about his efforts in his survey, published only two years after Rothenberg's first edition, of what was then available in anthologies of traditional Indian song. Bevis demonstrated substantial reasons for pinning his "Not Recommended" label on *Shaking the Pumpkin*, including this, on a series of "Sioux Metamorphoses" which Rothenberg in a note claimed to have "worked" from Francis Densmore's *Teton Sioux Music*:

> Try to find them. ... But I don't mind so much that Rothenberg covers his tracks; it's the direction he was taking when last seen. In blind attention to content, and total insensitivity to style and aesthetic form, such 'renderings' ... rival the worst anthropology (700).

McAllister saw nothing wrong in Rothenberg's use of Indian materials to promote "Beat, Projective, and Concrete" poetry, correctly pointing out that notions about traditional Indian song always have been affected by the literary fashions contemporary in the dominant white culture. Washington Matthews apparently was influenced by Whitman in his translation of the Navaho "Night Chant," and Mary Austin's notion of an "American rhythm" in traditional Indian song and Frances Densmore's versions of Chippewa song emerged in the context of the Imagism of the 1920's.

But Rothenberg's exploitation of Indian materials for the sake of his own doctrinaire assumptions about the nature of poetry was only one of his "literary offenses" charged in 1981 in a devastating article by William M. Clements, who demonstrated that Rothenberg also was guilty of shoddy scholarship and, even worse, misrepresentation of the intentions of Indian informants. Rothenberg claimed that he and his crew had produced "total translations," but Clements argued that if there is such a thing as "total translation" it derives from first-hand experience of the performance, close rapport with the performer, a sincere attempt to understand the "matrices" of the performance, and "deep respect for culture, performer, and performance." Without these conditions, he insisted, total translation becomes "gimmicky, ersatz, and counterproductive" (204).

Apparently Rothenberg did not read the Clements article because in 1986, as if we needed to be told that some people just cannot learn from their mistakes, he brought out a second edition of the book which, with few exceptions, merely put the same stuff forward -- and more of the same -- without apology.

Most of the "translations" in Rothenberg's anthology are only reworkings of the translations of others. To put it bluntly, an attribution like "English version by Jerome Rothenberg, after Harry Hoijer" (64) means that Rothenberg, believing that he knows better than Hoijer what poetry is, assumes that he knows better than Hoijer what the Indian -- a Navaho in this case -- was singing. But on what is this arrogance based? Hoijer, whatever he made of the song, at least knew the Navaho language. Does Rothenberg? His claim to greater authenticity actually is based on nothing more than his assumption that he is on to something about poetry, that the poetic process is universal, and that Hoijer's Navaho informant therefore *must* have meant to sing in Navaho something approximating Rothenberg's English.

What is most wearying about the second edition of *Shaking the Pumpkin* is Rothenberg's unwillingness to revise his commentaries in any substantial way or to correct the "literary offenses" cited by Clements. Fortunately he omitted one of the most outrageous "workings" Clements noticed: a "poem" about peyote which was actually his own abbreviated version of a Winnebago's prose description of his troubles with alcohol. Unfortunately whatever sensitivity caused him to junk this atrocity did not carry over to other examples cited by Clements, such as the brazen misquotation of James Mooney's translations of two Arapaho Ghost Dance songs. (Rothenberg's condescension toward the great achievements of Mooney, Densmore, Matthews, and others of their generation is one of the book's most obnoxious aspects, exceeded only by his smug assurance that he knows as well as Indians what they are up to when they sing.)

And if this is not bad enough, any reader more interested in the book's subject than its editor will be irritated by its editorial tone. Rothenberg's self-indulgent and eccentric commentaries and prefaces make clear that there is actually a network of people "working" Indian texts for all they are worth. For example, when I see a chummy reference to "Bill Merwin [working with] Plains Indian texts out of Lowie" (xxi) I assume that Rothenberg wants me to believe that W.S. Merwin has translated texts transcribed in the Crow language by Robert Lowie, but I know that what he actually means is that Merwin is busy making his own poems out of Lowie's literal translations of those transcriptions without knowing any more about the Crow language than I do. And of course the whole enterprise owes less allegiance to Indian tribal cultures than to Rothenberg's own critical agenda. When, for example, he calls a brief passage from a Seneca song "Two More About a Crow, in the Manner of Zukovsky," it's clear that he believes that the Seneca song does not mean much until it is propped up by allusion to Louis Zukovsky -- and, needless to say, by Jerome Rothenberg. And when he says, "The resemblance of Seneca verbal art to concrete & [sic] minimal poetry among us was another (if minor) point these translations were making" (349) we must be permitted to note that this point about "concrete & minimal poetry" was not minor at all: it is most of the reason for the existence of the anthology, and just as Paula Gunn Allen uses fiction by American Indian women to prove the premises of her radical feminism Rothenberg and his crew exploit songs Indians have gone to the trouble to sing -- as well as the work of those who went to the trouble to record and translate them -- to prove his premises about the nature of poetry.

What is most pathetic about this enterprise is that to cover the "concrete & minimal" dogmas which, though only mentioned in passing, are the real force that drives his book, he states intentions which are exactly right. Certainly one of the most essential tasks in Native American studies is the translation of traditional song into versions which reflect the tribal culture that created it and that culture's world view. But Rothenberg and his clique, for all their pretensions, seldom come anywhere near this ideal, and we are left too often with "poems" which scatter the alphabet around the page to make visual artifacts out of aural originals and with commentaries which for the most part were written not to explain the tribal culture which produced the originals -- about which Rothenberg probably does not know much anyway -- but to glorify the efforts of Rothenberg and his buddies to tell the unpoetic among us what poetry and thus Indian song are all about.

Another revealing Rothenberg performance, an anthology which he edited with Diane Rothenberg, *Symposium of the Whole: A Range of Discourse toward an Ethnopoetics* (1983), enshrines documents of the "ethnopoetics" movement (by Rothenberg himself, and by Charles Olson, Gary Snyder, Robert Duncan, George Quasha, and Victor Turner) with other materials, some of them related but many others only peripheral or merely fetched in to make the book look "scholarly." Of the pieces by Olson, Snyder, Duncan, Quasha, and Turner, one can only wonder how practitioners of the "ethnopoetics" racket can expect us to be impressed with their translations from other languages, to say nothing of their "reworkings" of pirated translations, when, if the prose the Rothenbergs have selected is any indication, they possess no apparent capacity for writing readable English. Quasha and Turner in particular, in spite of their posturing as rebels against received anthropology, commit the crime of jargon in a most traditional way.

The book includes basic pieces by writers whose contributions to the study of the "primitive" are universally acknowledged (Radin, Malinowski, Levi-Strauss, Whorf), as well as more recent discussions by Dell Hymes and Dennis Tedlock of the problems of translating primitive literatures. But some of the choices and omissions seem whimsical at best. For example, space was found for a piece on the sign language of the deaf but not for anything on the sign language of the American Indian. And though I must admit that I am unable to see what the transatlantic nonsense of Barthes and Derrida has to do with the premises of "ethnopoetics" -- or for that matter with anything else -- maundering examples of their stuff are tossed in, apparently to make the book look "up to date" -- in other words, merely fashionable. Furthermore a late eighteenth-century piece by Johann Gottfried Herder, significantly on the writings of James MacPherson ("Ossian"), who was himself a kind of Scottish "white shaman," apparently denies the entire enterprise of the "ethnopoetics" movement: "The human race is fated to a progression of scenes, cultures, and customs: woe to the man who is dissatisfied with the scene he is supposed to appear in ...!" (7) I think what Herder meant is what Geary Hobson and other Indian critics meant when they said that the "white shamans" rig themselves out as Indians because they know nothing about, and cannot relate to, their own culture or its antecedents. Hobson might have said the same thing about Rothenberg's gang.

In other words, the Rothenbergs' "symposium" is a cult book, flawed by ideological and doctrinaire excesses that are fatal to truly humanistic study, and as we slog through some of its selections we are left inescapably with a sense that we are eavesdropping on the private discussions of Rothenberg and his cronies. Unfortunately this absurd book, self-indulgent as it is, is by no means an uncharacteristic product of what too often passes for literary "scholarship" in our presently benighted culture.

If we examine more fully the state of editing and translating in the field of American Indian studies we will see that things need not be as bad as this. Joseph Bruchac, for the best example, has edited a series of anthologies of Indian writing which conform to the ideal which I have defined in relation to the achievement of Frank Hamilton Cushing and has provided for many of us our first encounter at an early stage of their careers with writers who later have proved significant. His *New Voices from the Longhouse* (1989), a collection of writings by Iroquois writers, and his *Raven Tells Stories* (1991), an anthology of writing by Eskimos and Alaska Indians, are models of how these things should be done. The authors and pieces he selects speak for themselves, and the only axe he seems to want to grind is on behalf of our greater understanding of Native American cultures.

As for translations I submit that probably the nearest we can come to an honest representation of what the original singers sang would be a combination of a sound recording of the singing with transcriptions in the original language, explanations of the structure and sound of that language and of the full context of the singing, transliterations of the songs in English, and readable literal English versions of those transliterations.

Lacking such translations, we can cite two examples which come very near to that ideal -- Leanne Hinton and Lucille J. Watahomigie's collection of Yuman texts (*Spirit Mountain*, 1984) and Nora and Richard Dauenhauer's program of collecting and translating everything that still remains of the traditional narratives and orations of the Tlingits.

Hinton and Watahomigie present a variety of texts from eight Yuman groups whose homelands are in Baja California and the valley of the lower Colorado River. Each group is given a general introduction, appropriate maps and photographs, biographical notes on informants, bibliographies and exact documentation of sources, explanations of the pronunciation system of the tribal language, and the texts themselves, with English translations -- and Spanish in a case from Baja California -- in parallel columns.

The Dauenhauers in two volumes of oral narratives and oratory -- *Haa Shuka, Our Ancestors* (1987) and *Haa Tuwunaagu Yis, for Healing Our Spirits* (1991) -- have collected not "rewrites" -- Rothenberg's racket -- but transcriptions of what, in each case, a single informant said on a specific occasion, with translations designed -- by means of layout, orthography, punctuation, and a thorough knowledge of Tlingit language, history, and culture -- to capture in English the quality of the original. These texts, along with a thorough introduction to their format, oral style, and cultural context, a thorough explanation of Tlingit phonetics and grammar, extensive historical and linguistic notes, and brief biographies of the informants, provide us with anthologies which are simultaneously works of literature, thoroughgoing contributions to scholarship, and acts of homage to the Tlingit elders who contributed to the project for the sake of their descendants.

These three books are profound additions to our understanding of American Indian culture, and because of their thorough and impeccable scholarship they may not seem glib and "smart" enough for those whose idea of real contributors to our knowledge of American Indian song is Jerome Rothenberg and his clique. But they give us a clear vision into the tribal culture of the people concerned, and those people emerge from our reading of the texts and the accompanying commentary as both fully tribal and fully human. Above all, the rationality of the scholarship is a blessing when compared to the implicit supernaturalism in Rothenberg's enterprise.

This point is worth making. Rothenberg and the "white shamans" apparently approach Indian cultures with the assumption that those cultures are most worth the attention of modern readers who, because they are "civilized," are ridden by the hags of rationality. The Indian, according to this notion, is free of all that has made Europeans -- or, more precisely, "Euro-Americans" -- so neurotic, "linear," "male-dominated," and so on. But if such an over-simplification tells us anything of value it ought to explain all Indian achievements, not just those that fit the theory. It is worth saying, in other words, that the most impressive thing about the structure of the Iroquois League, for example, is its great clarity and rationality. John Mohawk, in a piece collected in Bruchac's *New Voices from the Longhouse*, explains the traditions of Deganawidah, whose religious vision inspired the League, in terms of *rational* approaches to social and political problems. Perhaps the most telling event in the story of Deganawidah is what occurred when he and his disciple, Heyawentha, met Atataho, the Onandaga chief who was the last to take his people into the League and who, according to tradition, had snakes in his hair. Heyawentha combed them away in an act that may be understood as a metaphor for Atataho's recovery of sanity and for the final achievement of peace and rationality by the original five nations of the League. We cannot ignore the irony of this. In an age when our dominant culture often seems a self-indulgent flirtation with the most brainless forms of irrationality and supernaturalism and when a basic premise of that culture is that supernaturalism is justified by Indian example, John Mohawk argues that the spiritual foundations of the League were essentially rational because spirit and intellect, religion and political structure, mirrored each other in the Iroquois conception of things.

The fullness of this comprehensive vision of the League may stand as an ideal for anyone who approaches the culture of an Indian tribe, whether as anthropologist, translator, or editor. It is the full understanding of the culture that is needed, not only for the sake of an honest and honorable relation to a tribal people but for our understanding of those people -- and ourselves.

CHAPTER III

USING THE INDIAN: FOUR EXAMPLES

We have seen that translators and editors too often have used the American Indian as a symbolic figure to prove this or that premise of their own ideological or doctrinaire agendas. But this is hardly new in American experience. In American culture the Indian has been first an abstraction and only later, if at all, a person. As Louis Owens puts it, "[The] Indian in today's world consciousness is a product of literature, history, and art, and a product that, as an invention, often bears little resemblance to actual, living Native American people" (4). To a degree this is probably an inevitable result of minority status: either as enemy to be fought or as victim to be defended the Indian has been seen to stand for something, a kind of cardboard cut-out to be knocked down or set up by those who thought the country would be a better place if the "red devils" were exterminated or if the "vanishing American" were rescued by those who wanted to atone for the imperfections in the country's history.

And from the beginning the Indian has played a symbolic role in our literature. From Freneau's Indian in his grave to Leatherstocking's "red brother" to Berger's "Little Big Man" to Kevin Costner's Indians in "Dances with Wolves"-- the Sioux, that is, not the stereotypical "red devils" who are their Pawnee enemies -- the Indian has represented something our dominant culture has valued. Our next question, therefore, is how we might define legitimate and illegitimate uses of the American Indian as a subject. We may find an answer to this question by taking account of four writers of fiction who have dealt with Indians and their cultures.

Juanito Razon was a Cahuilla who until his death in 1927 lived in the Cahuilla homeland northwest of the Salton Sea in the California desert. He probably lived there most or even all of his long life -- perhaps a hundred years -- and he was known by his white neighbors as a kind of local character who was willing, for a fee, to pose for tourists' cameras in an army tunic and a top hat which he always wore "in town." For various reasons his public image was ambivalent. He was said to have found a secret gold mine and to have served as a scout for Fremont. Various rumors about a murderous past circulated along with true stories of his frequent kindnesses to lost travelers. And because he maintained an orchard of fig trees, he was known to everyone as Fig Tree John.

After Razon's death Edwin Corle, seeking a subject for his first novel, picked up various items of misinformation from local white people, including the notion that Razon actually was an Apache. This led him to research into Apache myth and tradition that was extensive enough to elicit the praise of no less a figure than the distinguished ethnologist Frederick Webb Hodge and to writing *Fig Tree John* (1935), which too many have assumed to have been based on the life of Juanito Razon. The novel was commercially successful, and it excited the enthusiasm of reviewers, who apparently assumed that Corle's considerable skill in narrative and characterization was due to deep awareness of "the Indian."

The facts of the case, however, have been available to the general reader since 1977, when the anthropologist Peter Beidler published all that apparently can be known of the details of Juanito Razon's life. Beidler examined the historical and ethnological materials upon which Corle based his novel and the differences between Razon's life and that of Corle's fictional character and defended the novel as a work of art in spite of those differences. The biographical details suggest that the fictional Fig Tree John is wildly at odds with the actual person upon whom Corle thought he was based. His character Agocho is a war comrade of Geronimo who comes to the Salton Sea area in 1906 with his young wife. They settle there, and she bears a son and later is raped and murdered by white outlaws. One of Corle's informants told him that Razon was disgusted when his son, Johnny Mack, "went white" and that he assumed sexual rights to Johnny's wife because Apaches, according to this informant, were polygamous. Needless to say, this is rather an odd idea of what *polygamy* means, and, also needless to say, an Apache knows as well as anyone else how to define *incest*. But this was the germ of the lurid catastrophe of Corle's novel. Agocho waits twenty years for the chance to avenge the death of his wife. Then Johnny Mack marries a Mexican girl, and Agocho concludes that the Apache gods have sent her as the means by which he may fulfill his vengeance. He rapes her and attempts to kill her. She runs away, but because she is carrying Johnny's child she writes to tell him to come to her. Agocho assaults Johnny's Ford with an axe to keep him from leaving, and Johnny kills him and drives away -- "gone white."

Very little in this ridiculous story makes any sense, and we can only be flabbergasted by the fact that even supposedly knowledgeable readers in 1935 were impressed with it. Agocho was not the first victim of a crime to want vengeance nor the first to seek it by committing his own crime against the innocent. But the notion that Apache mores about polygamous marriage and Apache religious notions of vengeance condoned a man's rape and attempted murder of his daughter-in-law is as simply preposterous as Agocho's apparent belief that he can "kill" a Ford with an axe. Agocho, in other words, cannot be understood as only one of "the wild and warlike Apaches, more or less typical of the Athapascan stock" to whom Corle referred in a letter quoted by Beidler (182). He's just crazy -- and he for sure is not Juanito Razon.

For Walter James Miller, who wrote the introduction to a 1971 reprint of the novel, Corle's "little classic" is relevant to present-day environmental concerns because Agocho's conception of the natural world is so eloquent a rebuke to the environmental blundering of modern America. But any reader who approaches the book without ideological preconceptions must conclude that Agocho is in fact the "wild and warlike" savage Corle imagined -- just another stereotypical "red devil." Corle is sympathetic with Agocho's sensitivity to the natural world and his devotion to what he calls "my land," and obviously the rape and murder of Agocho's wife are appalling. But the truth of the matter is that though Agocho, an Apache, claims that "this is all my land" no white man is any more than he a squatter on the land of the Cahuillas. And this natural man who actually does love the earth and actually is cruelly victimized by white brutes becomes by the end of the novel a lunatic who assumes that his daughter-in-law deserves to be raped and killed because she's white. He becomes, in short, a racist and a homicidal maniac, and Corle's only explanation for this is that the Apache gods make him do it.

By contrast, Juanito Razon's life, though less "exciting" than Agocho's and certainly lacking its lurid details, certainly reveals heroic elements. Whatever Corle's white informants told him, Razon was *not* a loner cut off from his people. He was, in fact, much involved with the life of the Cahuillas, and he took pride in their achievements, history, and lore. Unlike Agocho he possessed a legitimate title to the land he called his own, including a letter from Chief Cabazon of the Cahuillas naming him *Capitan* over the land where he lived and another from a California Indian commission confirming that title. To maintain his rights he retained a lawyer and used these documents to fight encroachment on his land not only by the Southern Pacific Railroad but also by his white neighbors, a fact which probably accounts for their lies about him. And he was successful. His long life, by any definition, was heroic and, considering that its events included many kindnesses to strangers, some of whom literally owed their lives to him, it was useful as well.

Corle -- unfortunately Beidler agrees with him -- assumed that such a life, however commendable, was not dramatic enough for a work of fiction. Thus the "exciting" rape, attempted murder, and patricide.

But the novel's commercial success was probably due not only to its sensationalism but to Corle's underlying theme, which he himself said was "assimilation." In 1953 he explained it in a letter:

My theme ... was the result of Fig Tree's running into white civilization .... The result meant the end of the Indian; in this case the race symbolized by Fig Tree himself. The next generation "goes white," and the son of Johnny Mack and Maria the Mexican girl will be entirely conditioned by white civilization. The orthodox Indian will die out (quoted by Beidler, p. 82).

One irony of modern American Indian life is that as the alleged Indian population increases to the satisfaction of the U.S. Census, Indians, willingly or unwillingly, realizing the fact or not realizing it, increasingly are being assimilated into the larger American society. Or to put it another way, more and more American citizens are claiming an Indian identity which, except for the most traditional tribal members on reservations, steadily means less and less, at least as far as racial and tribal identity are concerned. Assimilation, which sixty or seventy years ago was a question of policy to be debated, is now a reality in the evolution of American society and consciousness.

Leaving aside the question of whether this is a good or bad thing, it's clear that Corle believed that assimilation into the dominant white society was an appropriate goal for Indians. The thrust of his novel is that if Indians do not assimilate they will end up like Agocho, lost in the savagery of their origins and doomed. It's clear that, as far as he was concerned, Johnny Mack had no choice but to kill his father and that we are supposed to admire his flight toward assimilation. After all, we would not want him to end up like Agocho, in the insane grip of the Apache gods who are responsible for his murderous behavior. That pitiful savage just can't help himself. He's an Apache. It's the way "they" are.

Crazy Weather, the only novel by Charles L. McNichols, enjoyed favorable reviews and a substantial sale when it was published in 1944 and then was soon forgotten by critics and scholars. It is seldom mentioned in literary histories or bibliographies of American literature, and though it has appeared in a variety of editions the critical attention it deserves has unfortunately been deflected by a tendency to regard it as a juvenile.[1]

If *Crazy Weather* is a juvenile, then so is *Huckleberry Finn*. In fact it is significant both as a work of literature and as evidence that, regardless of its author's race, a work of fiction actually can do justice to Indian experience if it is informed by a thorough understanding of a tribal culture.

The Indians who figure in *Crazy Weather* are the Mojaves, who lived from prehistoric times in the Colorado Valley of California and Arizona. McNichols, while pursuing graduate study under the direction of Alfred Kroeber, thoroughly researched the Mojaves, and as the son of a special agent of the Department of the Interior he was raised on various Indian reservations in the West, including the Fort Mohave, which lies along twenty miles of the Arizona side of the Colorado below the tip of southern Nevada. His knowledge of Mojave life, in other words, was based both on personal experience and on systematic study.[2]

The Mojaves were a remarkable people for the many ways they were unlike most of the other Southwestern tribes, even those of their own Yuman linguistic family. They were primarily agriculturalists and gatherers, not hunters, but they also were extremely war-like, regarding war not as the last extremity (as did the pueblo dwellers) or as a source of loot (as did the Apaches) but as a means by which warriors could gain distinction. In this they resembled the Indians of the Plains, though they were not nomads.

They believed that they had been placed in the valley of the Colorado far back in the prehistoric darkness by Mastamho, their culture hero, who instituted their clan system, taught them the techniques of agriculture, and gave them their religion, which was unique for its emphasis on dreaming. Dreams were not, as among the Plains tribes, the results of deliberate acts such as fasting, isolation, vigils, or self-torture. To Mojaves the dreams came without bidding and were believed to be the cause of all events. A man who dreamed of being sick believed he would become sick. If he dreamed of wealth, he believed he would become wealthy. All of the myths and legends of the Mojaves were the products of the men who dreamed them. They dreamed of participating in the earliest history of the Mojaves; the dream was the result of the past making itself known in the present in the sleeping mind of the dreamer. We must take account of all of this if we are to comprehend the motivation of McNichols' protagonist and the novel's plot, which, given the likelihood that most readers have not read it, must be summarized.

The story McNichols tells is of South Boy, a fourteen-year-old who lives on a cattle-ranch near the Mojave reservation late in the first decade of the present century. (A reference to "that new song, 'Redwing'" fixes the date as being in or soon after 1907.) He is called South Boy by the Mojaves because he was born downriver from them, and though he is white he accepts his Mojave name and everything else Mojave. The action of the novel occurs during four days of "crazy weather," when the temperature rises above 110 degrees, insects die, horses flounder, and white men get sunstroke. It's a strange time, and it ends in rain and, for South Boy, in self-discovery.

South Boy is more or less alone on the ranch, casually supervised by the white foreman and his Mexican wife, because his mother is in Los Angeles recovering from surgery and his father is away on business. He is alone to struggle with his problem, which basically is one of having to decide whether to live like a white man or an Indian. He speaks fluent Mojave, and he usually thinks in Mojave terms, and he knows that if he decides to live as a white man he will be sent away to school. His mother wants him to be a Presbyterian minister -- as revolting an idea to South Boy as that of staying home to submit to the drudgery of ranch work and "responsibilities."

The only apparent alternative is the life of the Mojaves. South Boy accepts the invitation of his friend Havek to go upriver where "there's a very great *hota* holding a boys' sing." A *hota* is a wise man, a singer and interpreter of dreams. South Boy takes a little food and digs out from under the house a mail-order revolver which he has kept concealed and which he carries thereafter inside his shirt as a secret even from Havek, thinking of it as "only a sort of talisman" like a Mojave's "medicine."

Clearly for Havek the journey is more than a vacation: he is going to war. He has heard of "trouble" to the north with the Piutes, and this will provide the setting for his discovery of his new name. Actually his name *Havek* is his mother's joke. It means *two* and his mother called him that because she thought she was going to have twins when she was carrying him. In other words his name -- like South Boy's -- implies a lack of identity which can be remedied only with some heroic act of warfare by which he can be known in the future.

So Havek and South Boy go north to the "sing." There one of the Mojave boys sings the Mojave creation myth, and when he tells of the death and cremation of a Mojave god, the other boys weep, while South Boy, unable to weep, feels separate from them. The next day he and Havek continue north to the camp of the Whisperer, a skilled maker of bows and arrows, and there South Boy meets a sister of Heepa, the Mojave woman who nursed him as a baby and who is therefore his "deputy foster mother ...." Traveling further they see Yellow Road, a great-uncle of Havek and the last of the great Mojave warriors, who tells them stories of his exploits and announces that "the days of our greatness are ended." Yellow Road tells him that he will die if he does not get "big meat" -- in this case wild horse -- and South Boy takes Yellow Road's rifle and shoots a beautiful wild horse and then is sickened by what he has done.

The next day they find two horses lost by a Piute whose behavior, judging by the "sign" he has left, is incomprehensible. Havek concludes that the man is crazy, and when they ride the horses to a ghost town they find that South Boy's friend, who is called the Mormonhater, has been attacked by the Piute and knifed in the leg. The Mormonhater is a freethinking follower of Robert Ingersoll because his various religious beliefs (Mormon, Catholic, Protestant, and Indian) have canceled each other out. But he has remained extremely superstitious, and he tells the boys that the Piute is a witch and that his "medicine" must be destroyed before the sun shines on it the next morning or it will mean the end of the world. Obviously the Mormonhater is as cracked as the Piute, but his ravings make sense to South Boy and Havek. Before sun-up they go forth to war. In a wild and disjointed melee they attack and are attacked by the Piute, who escapes by jumping in the river as South Boy blasts away with his mail-order revolver. "Well," he says, "if this is what they call war, to hell with it ...." But then as he destroys the Piute's "medicine" (and presumably saves the world) Havek, whose name is now Hawk Strikes because of his courage against the Piute, sees the "medicine" before it can be burned. "Some of it entered the boy," the Mormonhater explains, and Havek is "witch-struck." When South Boy sees the Mormonhater employ all of his own "medicine," Piute, Mojave, Catholic, and Protestant -- none of it with success -- he is so impressed that he asks him to make him his disciple, but the Mormonhater advises him to learn about railroads and irrigation.

So South Boy takes Havek home, meeting on the way a Mojave medicine man who cures Havek simply by telling him that the Mormonhater's witch-talk was only "a great foreign nonsense" and that the great Yellow Road is dying. When they get to Yellow Road's camp the mourning has begun. Because the Mojaves cremate their dead as soon after death as possible, a Mojave policeman from the agency arrives to make sure that Yellow Road actually is dead before the fire is lit. South Boy, who feels himself to be in "a vacuum between two worlds," finds an ideal in Joe the policeman because as a graduate of the Indian school at Haskell, Kansas, he has learned how to live in the Mojave world and the white man's world at the same time. South Boy is determined to go to Haskell to learn how to do this and disappointed when Joe tells him that he can't because he's not an Indian.

The four days of "crazy weather" have enabled South Boy to pick a new name for himself, but he feels lost. Then it begins to rain, and in the violence of the storm he hears the Mojave boys "throwing away their dreams" in expectation of death. In this crisis South Boy believes that his mother's Presbyterian God is passing judgment on him, and he passes out, finding when he awakes that the "crazy weather" is over. The air is cool, and the earth is soggy with rain. Now he realizes what he must do. He takes leave of Havek -- and of Mojave ways -- and goes back to the ranch with a great plan for buying up as many cattle as possible and grazing them on the mesa, which the rain has made unseasonably verdant. He knows that he now must cut his hair, wear boots, and use a saddle, but he's glad to do it and he sets forth to become rich.

As with so many Indian cultures -- virtually all of them in fact -- the magic number for the Mojaves was *four*. In *Crazy Weather* Havek and South Boy each go to war with the Piutes with only four war arrows for their bows. The old medicine man tells the boys that "a spider was spinning her trails around Yellow Road's head .... If she makes three roads, it's bad. If she finishes the fourth before I can stop her, the old man is dead." And after four days of "crazy weather" South Boy reaches wisdom.

Four also structures the plot of the novel. At the beginning South Boy believes he must choose among three worlds which his mother has defined for him. One is the world of "Cultural Advancement and Christian Instruction" which she represents. "Certainly she was no part of either of the two worlds around her -- ... the Rough world of the White Man and the Heathen World of the Indian." South Boy's journey away from both "Another World" and "the Rough World" to "the Heathen World" ends in the magical *fourth* world of maturity and responsibility.

This use of *four* to structure South Boy's journey to maturity can also be seen in his attempts to emulate first the Mojaves, then the Mormonhater, then Joe the policeman. The Mojave thesis and the Mormonhater's antithesis seem to be synthesized in Joe the policeman, whose double consciousness seems ideal to South Boy: "You can figure things out white way and Indian way both [and not] get caught in the middle ...." But this synthesis is unavailable to South Boy because, not being an Indian, he cannot go to Haskell to learn how to achieve it. The thesis, the antithesis, and the synthesis of the two are all impossible for him. The magical solution is the fourth road, which South Boy earns to walk alone.

In terms of subject, plot and structure, *Crazy Weather* is a unified work in large part because of the thorough understanding of the Mojave experience which informs it. The failure of students of American literature to take account of it is unfortunate, given its maturity as a treatment of the Indian in American fiction. The story of the white boy who runs away from civilization with his Indian brother appears often in our cultural history, from Natty Bumpo to the Lone Ranger, but McNichols tells a more mature story than either of these. His hero rejects his mother's culture and Christianity, but he also rejects both the world of the Mojaves and any attempt to reconcile it with his mother's world. For him there are four, not three, worlds that may be sought: Indian, white, a synthesis of the two, and his own fourth way, which is not only South Boy's personal vision but also McNichols' vision of the end of received notions of the reality of the American West. The Mormonhater, the ranch foreman who dreams of Buffalo Bill's show-business Wild West, and the last Mojave warrior Yellow Road all tell South Boy that the West has come to the end of something and to the beginning of something else.

McNichols' attitude toward all this can be seen in a funny short story, "The Buck in the Brush," which dates from the time of the publication of *Crazy Weather*. It tells of a missionary, Miss Daisybelle Stacey, who is rescued from drowning in the Colorado River by a "locoed" Indian who regards her as salvage and demands to sleep with her. She runs away to Los Angeles, and when the story's narrator visits her he finds her reading *Hiawatha* beneath "a picture of such a fancy-looking Indian as never was born." That says it all. *Hiawatha* and the ersatz Indian maid in "Redwing," which South Boy hears the Mojaves singing on the reservation, derive from the white man's culture which South Boy rejects in the name of freedom with responsibilty, an act which, for McNichols, typifies the writer who is determined to examine the reality, rather than the myth, of the American Indian. In this respect, *Crazy Weather* is an important document in our cultural history.

When we put *Fig Tree John* and *Crazy Weather* side by side the comparison is telling. They suggest that when non-Indian writers deal with tribal cultures they go wrong when they attempt to depict an Indian point of view by portraying Indian protagonists, as Corle did, from the inside out, so to speak, because this strategy inevitably produces symbolic figures who falsify or at least over-simplify the Indian experience they claim to portray. By committing himself to assimilation as an ideal, Corle made this bad matter worse. On the other hand, when Indian characters and their tribal culture are presented from the outside as the background for a white character's story both the culture and its people may remain human rather than symbolic. What redeems *Crazy Weather* and damns *Fig Tree John* is that McNichols did not want to use his Mojave subject to prove anything about it. He neither praises nor condemns it. South Boy's rejection of the Mojave way does not mean that it is worthless but that he can achieve neither it nor his mother's "Cultural Advancement and Christian Instruction" nor any reconciliation of the two.

Perhaps another way to define the difference between the two novels is to say that Corle's tragic vision of the Indian "problem" is "serious" while the story McNichols tells is comic and utterly devoid of social "message." Indeed they seem to suggest the wisdom of Gerald Vizenor's contention that the comic mode is most appropriate for writing by and about Indians because it avoids the dead-end despair that is the inevitable product of literary portrayals of the Indian as "vanishing American." We may understand the implications of Vizenor's argument by taking account of his work and of what seems to me to be artistically the most successful work of comic literature yet produced by an Indian writer -- Thomas King's *Green Grass, Running Water* (1993).

An important work in any case, King's novel combines with remarkable ingenuity an impressive variety of narrative skills, a keen satiric sense, and a wide knowledge of traditional American Indian cultures, setting a high standard for the future as the first major Indian novel which is unabashedly comic in its intentions.

The novel's subject -- more or less -- is the collapse of a dam in Alberta which has flooded ancestral Blackfoot lands. Eli, who has led a white man's existence professing English in Toronto, has returned to his inheritance and lives in his mother's house in the face of the "progress" which the dam represents. His nephew Lionel is a television salesman who has had an affair with Alberta, who teaches frontier history in a university in Calgary to students who care nothing at all for the subject. She wants to conceive a child, but not with Lionel or with her other lover, Charlie, a lawyer who represents the interests of the power company which built the dam. Meanwhile Latisha runs the Dead Dog Cafe, selling her various dishes as dog meat to tourists who demand them as "authentic" ethnic cuisine. These characters, all Canadian Blackfeet, go to a Sun Dance, and then the dam collapses.

Their stories provide the novel's satiric vision of the complexities of Indian life in North America; but equally significant is another story, strange and mythic, of the adventures of four ancient Indians who escape from a mental hospital south of the border, go to Alberta to destroy the dam with magic which is not specified but apparently works, and return to the hospital when they have succeeded. Their psychiatrist believes that they may be centuries old and responsible for every natural disaster in their lifetimes. Their names -- Lone Ranger, Ishmael, Robinson Crusoe, and Hawkeye -- and the implied relationship of these four names to Tonto, Queequeg, Friday, and Chingachgook suggest the interrelationship of European and Indian, or at least non-white, elements in our culture and reveal King's cosmopolitan understanding not only of literature in general but of many Indian mythologies, with Christian, Indian, and literary elements informing one another in new myths which are themselves comic masterpieces. As an example of King's mythological fireworks, one whacky story tells of First Woman, both a Navaho founding mother and a cognate of the Biblical Eve, who creates land out of a watery world and then a garden in which she lives with her husband Ahdamn, who names, or rather misnames, everything. Food falls from a tree when she bumps into it, and then God shows up and they leave the garden to escape his divine belly-aching and run into "rangers," who shoot at them until First Woman puts on a mask and passes off Ahdamn and herself as Tonto and the Lone Ranger.

King's novel is a permanent addition to the corpus of American Indian literature which will serve as a benchmark in the history of that subject. It is, that is to say, the comic masterpiece that a reader of Gerald Vizenor's theoretical writings might expect to be produced sooner or later. Against the background of the frequent references to Coyote and Trickster by American Indian writers, Vizenor has contended that the true Indian vision is comic. His own experiments in fiction have shown him to be the only Indian writer to employ the methods of the "post-modern" novel, to abandon the "air of reality" of the realist and the symbolism of the modernist and to regard fiction as a kind of artistic game. As far as he is concerned, the only strategy for the Indian writer is comedy because comedy is compatible with an Indian vision of community and tribe while traditional tribal narratives are only the inevitably tragic remnants of dying cultures.

In *Manifest Manners: Postindian Warriors of Survivance* (1994), a collection of essays on the American Indian's present social, political and cultural state, Vizenor attempts to make some legitimate complaints against reservation gambling casinos, certain phony Indian "activists," the falsification of Indian experience by mainstream American culture, and so on   But in the process he contrasts traditional tribal storytelling with "the classical notion that thoughts [are] representations of content, or the coherent meaning of words..." (72).   One wonders how a traditional tribal story -- or any other for that matter -- can get anywhere if its words are incoherent, but that may not be what Vizenor is saying. Or is he? The truth is that a reading of his essays leaves the reader wondering just what he really is saying. Apparently bemused by odd notions which he justifies as "post-modern," he proceeds in a style -- if that's the word for it -- which seems to be the product of an assumption that if content has nothing to do with thought in a traditional story and that if a traditional storyteller is permitted to use incoherent language which need not communicate anything *but* its incoherence then there is no reason why a "scholar" should not have the right to use equally meaningless and incoherent language. It is worth noting that the above statement is embedded in almost two pages of quotations strung together with little comment and that the addled reader is left suspecting that in spite of modish allegiance to supposedly advanced ideas the academy today is grinding out as much muddled writing as it ever did.   Indeed Vizenor's citation of one Richard

Wolin's explanation of Foucault's comment on Derrida's "[leading] us into the text from which ... *we never emerge*" (71) suggests that he may expect his readers to wander around in his linguistic maze without ever returning to a world where most people -- some of them even professing English in universities -- try to say clearly what they mean. For example, one of the essays, on "Shadow Survivance," begins with two sentences which may be -- I must admit that I cannot tell -- the thesis statement for the essay. What, may I ask, do they mean?

> The postindian turns in literature, the later indication of new narratives, are an invitation to the closure of dominance in the ruins of representation. The invitation uncovers traces of tribal survivance, trickster hermeneutics, and the remanence of intransitive shadows (63).

We may be tempted to conclude that *Manifest Manners* is just one more example of the academic celebration of jargon, some of it in fact apparently made up by the author under the misguided notion that what is wrong with the jargon already proving a great bore in our graduate schools is that there's not enough of it. But when we remember that Vizenor believes that the true Indian vision is comic we may wonder if the book itself, though published by a university press and decorated with a couple of endorsements by academics -- one of them Thomas King, of all people -- might be intended as a great joke, a spoof of the worst excesses of academic self-indulgence. Perhaps that explains it. But if it does, the joke is less on defenders of clear prose than on those of us who really do believe that it matters whether Indian tribes maintain their social and cultural integrity.

The truth is that Vizenor, when he feels like it, can write clearly enough. *The Everlasting Sky* (1972), his book about the present-day Chippewa of Minnesota, is a readable book -- because of its intended audience, presumably, or perhaps because of more determined editing -- and his fiction, for all of its quirkiness, is comprehensible. For example, the fourteen stories collected in *Landfill Meditation* (1991) are, like his other fictions, readable (and funny) applications of his theories of "post-modern" narrative. They feature a kind of private lexicon and a characteristic blurring of autobiographical and fictional elements. His story "Almost Browne" is characteristic. Its protagonist was named Almost because he was almost brown (and almost white) and was almost born on an Indian reservation when his parents -- a blonde mother and a Chippewa father -- ran out of gas on their way to the reservation hospital. This story is placed appropriately first in the book because the word *almost* is basic to an understanding of Vizenor's methods: his fictions are almost stories, almost fictional, almost real. One of his characters says, "People are almost stories, and stories tell almost the whole truth," and another says, "The almost world is a better world, a sweeter dream than the world we are taught to understand in school." The almost world is that of the trickster or of the writer who "plays games with words in stories" because wit and imagination are the only appropriate creative response to a world which is changing and apparently going out of control.

This is at the heart of a justification of Vizenor's comic and experimental narrative methods, along with the scepticism he consistently applies to received notions. Inevitably preoccupied with mixed racial heritage as the descendant of Chippewa and French ancestors, he takes account of all of them, challenges even the most fashionable generalizations about Indians, and distrusts zealots in any cause. (For example, he recognized early that the leaders of the American Indian Movement [AIM], regardless of the legitimacy of their arguments, were basically television performers.)

In another story, "Feral Lasers," Almost Browne creates "postshamanic laser holotropes" which hover over the reservation. Then, banned by his tribe, he goes to the city to project feral lasers (bears and other animals) over the interstate highway. These "feral lasers" are Almost's adaptations of the technology of the modern world as a means of defeating it with its own tools. They are, that is, similar to the nonrealism, the wordplay, and the absurdity of the post-modern novel, as opposed to the elegiac "realism" of those writers, white and Indian alike, who mourn the passing of tribal identity and the loss of environmental concern for "mother earth," sentiments which, heard so often, are in danger of becoming cliches.

As for his nonfictional writings, there is no reason to doubt as we read them his sincerity in addressing contemporary Indian problems, even if what he is really getting at much of the time can only be pried out with great difficulty from the muddle he apparently feels compelled to create. But as we slog our way through his linguistic swamp we may be tempted to conclude that his "post-modernism" is more important to him than the predicament of the Chippewas or any other Indian tribe.

Still Vizenor's fiction justifies itself by often being quite funny, and King's novel is frequently hilarious. Whether or not Vizenor is right in his contention that the most appropriate mode for the Indian writer of fiction is comic, much of his own fiction suggests that he may be right and King's brilliant novel certainly vindicates the claim. In any case, Vizenor is exactly right in his assertion that the most appropriate inspiration for American Indian fiction derives from a traditional Indian vision of community and tribe, and the works to which we now must turn can be understood in the light of that inspiration and also may enable us to suggest a tentative definition of an American Indian literary tradition.

NOTES

1   *Crazy Weather* appeared in several printings of the original edition, in a British edition, in Swedish, German, and Japanese translations, and in a reprint by the University of Nebraska Press (Lincoln, 1967). It was published in a new edition by Viking Press in 1978. Stanley Vestal calls it "one of the best Southwestern juveniles" in *Book Lover's Southwest* (Norman: University of Oklahoma Press, 1955), p. 210.

2   For the life of McNichols and documentation of the sources of his novel in his own experience and in the ethnology of the Mojave, including elements in the novel which I will not discuss here, see my article, "Charles L. McNichols and *Crazy Weather*: A Reconsideration," *Western American Literature* 6 (Spring 1971): 39-51.

CHAPTER IV

TOWARD DEFINITION OF A LITERARY TRADITION

Any definition of an American Indian literary tradition will probably derive from an assumption that its origins inevitably must be found in traditional tribal definitions of reality. But when we proceed according to this assumption we immediately encounter difficulties in determining what the multitude of tribal cultures, even if we take account only of those still in existence, have in common.

As a hypothesis for approaching this subject I suggest that the one element which appears in every one of the hundreds of tribes that maintained their independence from each other when they first encountered Europeans is the pervading symbolic importance of the number *four* in explanations of the origin of the world and the tribe and in definitions of human nature and the natural world.

The ethnology of the American Indian includes too many examples of the symbolic use of the number *four* to catalogue here. Many Southwestern tribes assume that this world is the magical fourth world into which the first people emerged after ascending from three worlds below ours. The "earth-diver" origin myth found in tribes in most of the rest of North America frequently includes the assumption that birds or animals were only successful on a fourth attempt to dive to the bottom of the primordial sea to bring up a bit of mud out of which the Creator was able to shape the island which became the earth's primeval continent. Whereas

European folk-tales consistently deal with three brothers or sisters and with success that is achieved on a magical third attempt -- "The third time's the charm" -- the magical number of people or spirits or attempts in American Indian legend and myth is four.

Even more significantly, tribal cultures again and again define space and time in terms of four elements. The four directions are assumed to define not only the circle of the horizon but the circle of the four turning seasons and also the recurrent journey of the sun from its rising in the east through its height of noon and its setting in the west to its return through darkness to a new rising.

We may take as a starting-point for understanding this four-fold definition of reality the quaternity of the four directions as the Sioux holy man Black Elk described it to John G. Neihardt and as Neihardt edited it for the third chapter of *Black Elk Speaks* (1932).

At this point it must be remembered that the accuracy of Neihardt's transcriptions and his use of them in writing his book have been subjected to considerable analysis, and the book has been criticized as less an expression of Black Elk's vision and experience than of Neihardt's own European and white American preconceptions.

Any response to the charge that Neihardt falsified Black Elk's vision for his own artistic and philosophical purposes must take account of two factors. In the first place, with the publication of Raymond DeMallie's *The Sixth Grandfather* (1984) Neihardt's transcriptions are available to the general reader, and though the problem is complicated by the fact that the transcriptions are Neihardt's version of stenographic records of the rough English into which Black Elk's son translated what his father said in Lakota, the reader of DeMallie's book can decide to what extent, if any, Neihardt falsified what Black Elk told him. In the second place, much of the confusion about the remarkable mixture of "Euro-American" and Lakota elements in *Black Elk Speaks* must be attributed not to Neihardt's falsification of his source but to the remarkable mixture of Roman Catholic and Lakota elements in Black Elk's own life and vision. Black Elk, through most of his life, was more than a practicing Catholic; he was a successful and dedicated catechist respected for his work as a missionary among the Lakota. In other words, much of the rather Platonic conception of the relationship of this imperfect world to that in which, he believed, six "grandfathers" showed him an ideal of harmony which he was expected to bring back to his people derives not from Neihardt's reworking of what Black Elk told him but from the original vision as his understanding of it evolved through a lifetime of thought which inevitably was affected by his own Christian faith.

But what may be the most remarkable thing about Black Elk's vision, given his devotion to his Roman Catholic faith, is that in spite of the pervasive presence of trinity in Christian thought he retained the original vision's consistent emphasis upon quaternity. Furthermore, that emphasis may be found not only in Neihardt's book but in the transcriptions which Neihardt prepared in the context of his interviews with Black Elk and which are fully reprinted by DeMallie.

In any case, as Alice B. Kehoe has pointed out, Black Elk's fusion of Lakota and Roman Catholic religious elements in *Black Elk Speaks* and Joseph Epes Brown's account, in *The Sacred Pipe* (1953), of Black Elk's retelling of the myths which underlie seven Lakota ceremonies have profoundly influenced thinking about American Indian religion, even the thinking of many Indians: "Unquestionably this syncretism has been instrumental in establishing Black Elk's version of Oglala supernaturalism as *the* Indian religion" (197). Though Kehoe may be over-stating the case, this claim certainly suggests the possibility that a summary of Black Elk's version of quaternity might provide a starting-point for defining an American Indian literary tradition according to the quaternary terms of his vision.

We also should remember that the element of quaternity in the perception of the seasons, the landscape, the ages of man, and the natural world is pervasive in Lakota thought. William K. Powers has made the point that the inter-relatedness of space and time is clearly implied in the derivation of the Lakota word *omaka* (*year*) from the word for *earth* (*maka*), and he has documented an extensive list of Lakota quaternary definitions of the natural world, the passage of time, the elements of human character, and philosophical and religious concepts (48, 169).

Black Elk's vision was the basis for his belief that nature is circular, that, as he put it, all natural things try to be round, that time's measurements inevitably take form in the circle of nature, and that the basic symbol of nature and time is the circle of the horizon defined as the quaternity of the four directions. The basic wisdom of this conception is clear enough: we hear echoes of it in our most elementary figures of speech, as in our reference to "the wheel of time" or in our saying that "the years rolled by."

But the four directions are not only a way of understanding the horizon of the world's circle and the recurrence of time which that circle symbolizes. It also defines man's place in that world. The south is the direction of growing things, Black Elk said, and of "the power to grow." The west is associated with both creation and destruction because it is the direction of both lightning and the life-giving rain. The north is the source of winter storms, which Black Elk associated with human endurance. The east, because it is the direction of the morning star of "understanding" and the rising of the divine sun, symbolizes wisdom and spirituality.

What seems clear in this structure is that the two axes -- east-west and north-south -- are coherent representations of the interrelationship of man and nature. If *north* suggests human endurance and strength of character, *south* suggests growth and strength of body. On the other hand, the east-west axis opposes the spiritual wisdom of the sun and morning star to the creative and destructive powers of the natural world. Or, to put it another way, the two lines define man (mind and body) in relation to external reality (spirit and matter). Furthermore, Black Elk associated the four directions with the four ages of man and the four seasons, so that the circle from the east through the south and west to the north is a symbol of the journey from infancy through youth and maturity to old age and from spring through summer and fall to winter.

If the preoccupation with quaternity in the traditional vision of Indian tribes is relevant for a tentative definition of an American Indian literary tradition, we may test that relevance by considering three novels -- N. Scott Momaday's *House Made of Dawn* (1968), James Welch's *Winter in the Blood* (1974), and Leslie Marmon Silko's *Ceremony* (1977), as well as the work in which Momaday paid homage to his Kiowa forbears, *The Way to Rainy Mountain* (1969).

Momaday's career as a writer is the result of an interesting mix of Indian and non-Indian influences. A thorough-going scholar who studied at Stanford with Yvor Winters, wrote a doctoral dissertation on the nineteenth century New England poet Frederick Goddard Tuckerman, and edited a collected edition of that poet's work, he also is the son of a Kiowa father and a mother of mixed Cherokee and white ancestry. His parents worked as teachers on Indian reservations, and when Momaday was a boy he lived for several years at the pueblo of Jemez. *House Made of Dawn* is set largely on a reservation which clearly is Jemez, and the ritual life which it describes is that which Momaday saw there. On the other hand, his knowledge of Jemez history almost certainly was enhanced by his reading of Elsie Clews Parsons' study of *The Pueblo of Jemez* (1925), and the title of his novel derives from a familiar line from the Navaho *Night Chant*. Momaday's Indian background, in other words, is eclectic -- part-Cherokee in race but apparently uninspired by Cherokee tradition, part-Kiowa and profoundly affected by Kiowa tradition which he knows both from family stories and by study, familiar both through experience and from his reading with the culture of Jemez, author of a book with a title derived from Navaho ritual, thoroughly educated in the American and British literary traditions.

The interrelationship of Kiowa and Anglo-American elements informs *The Way to Rainy Mountain*, one of the most distinguished examples in American Indian literature of a writer's presentation of a tribal culture in a form which does justice to that culture while imprinting on it the author's own artistic stamp.

The mixed origins of the book are revealed in the fact that though Momaday deals with traditional Kiowa material which is authenticated both by scholarship and by memories of his grandmother's story-telling, its structure and at least some of the philosophical premises which inform it derive not from traditional Indian sources but from Momaday's literary education.

The Way to Rainy Mountain may be understood as a kind of prose poem derived from traditional materials which are perceived personally, an exercise in self-definition made possible by a definition of the tribal experience of the Kiowas. But ultimately the book's subject must be understood as language itself -- its origins, its power, its inevitable collapse, and finally its rebirth as art.

Momaday's conception of language may be understood in the light of the implications of Emerson's remark (in *Nature*) that every word was originally a poem, arising out of a need for some means of referring to a concrete phenomenon: *spirit*, for example, originally meant "wind." But the word, which begins as metaphor, becomes, through common usage, a cliche and finally sinks into the common earth of denotation. Yet words are the only means by which the poet can give meaning to reality, achieve self-definition, and in the process restore vitality to the words.

The structure which outlines this progress of language in *The Way to Rainy Mountain* is not in four parts, as one familiar with the pervasive quaternities in Indian legend and myth might expect, but in three. The three main divisions of the book -- "The Setting Out," "The Going On," and "The Closing In" -- may be understood in the conventional terms of beginning, middle, and end, or perhaps, more precisely, of birth, life, and death -- the origins, heyday, and final decline of the Kiowas as an independent people. Furthermore, each of the twenty-four sections which compose those three divisions is in three parts. Each includes a traditional Kiowa story, remembered by Momaday from his childhood experience with his grandmother, a historical commentary on the story, much of it derived from James Mooney's *Calendar History of the Kiowa Indians* (1898), and a personal, autobiographical statement about the experience which expresses the author's understanding of his own identity as an inheritor of Kiowa tradition. These three elements -- Kiowa myth, Kiowa reality, and personal vision -- may perhaps be understood as Kiowa soul, Kiowa body, and Kiowa (that is, the author's) mind. Clearly this division into three elements owes more to Momaday's literary education than to his Kiowa traditions.

But the primary consideration in the book's structure is that the three divisions reveal a movement from *myth* (the origins of the Kiowas and of their religious definition of themselves as a people) through *legend* (the stories of Kiowa freedom and prosperity as they told them to each other) to *history* (the factual account of the defeat of the Kiowas and of their fall into the reality of the workaday world). This process also may be understood in relation to the movement of language from poetry (metaphor) through cliche to mere denotation and, in the hands of the poet, back to poetry again and also in relation to a similar movement in the origins and evolution of myth. A myth arises out of a people's need for some means of defining their relationship to the world, seen and unseen. But through frequent re-telling it becomes a legend, begins to lose its original significance, and finally falls to earth under the weight of historical fact. The myth and its variants in legend and its parallels in history are the material of *The Way to Rainy Mountain* and the means by which its author, in the process of restoring vitality to the material, discovers his own relation to the Kiowa experience which produced the material in the first place.

Both in the Platonic premises of the book and in traditional Kiowa culture, language and religious vision are related, for, as Momaday says, "the word is sacred .... When Aho saw or heard or thought of something bad, she said the word *zei-dl-bei*, 'frightful.' ... It was ... an exertion of language upon ignorance and disorder."

A word, in other words, possesses power. "It comes from nothing [and] gives origin to all things." Indeed it gives man his only real power to "deal with the world on equal terms."

In the first section, "The Setting Out," the mythical stories deal, for the most part, with language and its power to work magic. They express a basic theme: the Kiowas originate in nature, from which they must separate to become a people and to acquire a tribal name and the elements of religious worship. Presumably this is what is meant by the myth of the domestication of the dog. As in the myths of so many peoples, it is a story of a time when animals could talk; but we are not to assume that this was a time when animals could speak Kiowa but a time when Kiowas could only speak the language of animals -- that is, before they became Kiowas.

In "The Going On" the stories are concerned with history and with the prosperity of the Kiowas, with escape from enemies and from natural disaster, with reconciliation of tribal conflict, with freedom, and with the horses which make freedom possible.

Finally, in "The Closing In," there is a steady decline from the freedom and power of the middle section to death and loss. The defeated Kiowas lose most of their horses and must eat others because buffalo are scarce, a great horse is stolen ("a hard thing to bear"), a medicine bundle becomes heavy when it is not shown proper respect, and so on. In all of these stories the content is increasingly historical, and the defeat, humiliation, and loss which they detail is made inevitable by the inability of the people to work their magic by means of the old language formulas.

Accompanying this story of the origins, rise and fall of the Kiowa people is the story of the author's discovery of himself *as* a Kiowa. In each of the twenty-four sections, divided among the three divisions in the Kiowa journey, the legend and its historical definition receive a personal interpretation. The journey of the Kiowas from the mountains of their origins to the final place of rest in the Rainy Mountain cemetery parallels the author's journey, through memory, from his first sight of the Great Plains to the final vision of the Rainy Mountain toward which the Kiowas were inevitably, and tragically, destined to find their way. The book is in part a record of the process by which the author became a Kiowa by discovering the relation of his memory and experience to the Kiowas of myth, legend, and history. The journey to Rainy Mountain is the Kiowa journey from their northern origins to their destiny on the southern plains, but it is also the author's own journey from his first discovery of what it means to be a Kiowa descendant to the recognition of common mortality with the Kiowa dead in the Rainy Mountain cemetery and of a final wisdom which makes possible the structuring of Kiowa tribal experience in a work of art.

The reader who sees little more in *The Way to Rainy Mountain* than a collection of scraps from a broken culture's mythology, legends, and history should remember that a casual reader might level the same charge against Eliot's *The Waste Land*. In fact, one of the last lines of Eliot's poem -- "These fragments I have shored against my ruins" -- suggests Eliot's strategy: to combine fragments of Europe's literary culture from Homer to our own century in new juxtapositions which define his own relation to that tradition. Momaday's strategy is not unlike this. The scraps of language which make up his book are structured coherently to form a unified vision out of autobiography and Kiowa history, legend and myth. That unity of Kiowa past and present, of Kiowa myth and reality, and of the Kiowa experience and the experience of one modern Kiowa, Momaday, is achieved in the only way that remains once the old vitality of the culture has fallen into memory -- by the ordering intelligence of the artist, which restores life to the myths of the Kiowas as it makes yet another contribution to the necessary restoration of life to language itself. Language, in Momaday's vision, verified both by Kiowa tradition and by its Platonic implications, is the magical element in human experience.

In other words, beyond the three stages of the Kiowa journey -- rise, heyday, and decline; myth, legend, and history -- there is a fourth stage, the realm of art. Momaday chose to structure his book in the light of a "European" emphasis upon trinity -- "Setting Out," "Going On," and "Closing In" -- but *The Way to Rainy Mountain* is itself the fourth stage, the artist's personal stage of poetry, of the art which reorganizes the myths, legends, and history of the Kiowas into a new artistic totality. It is the magical fourth stage of wisdom which, in Black Elk's terms, is implied in our understanding of a year's circle which begins in summer and moves through fall and winter to rebirth in the spring.

House Made of Dawn, on the other hand, is explicitly structured in four parts. Part I ("The Longhair") is set in a pueblo, which is fictitious but is clearly based on Jemez, during two weeks in the summer of 1945, when Abel, the protagonist, has just returned from military service in Europe. The "longhair" is Francisco, Abel's grandfather, and this section deals with Francisco's loss of Abel, who arrives home drunk, has an affair with a white woman, and is finally defeated in the festival rooster-pull by a frightening albino whom he later kills in a knife fight. This section is set seven years earlier than the other three, and it is dominated by Abel's memories of the death of his brother, his killing of a captured ceremonial eagle because of his disgust at its imprisonment, and his traumatic battle experiences. It also deals with the past of the pueblo, and in particular with the legendary origins of its summer festival.

Part II ("The Priest of the Sun") is set in Los Angeles in the winter of 1952, when Abel has been released from prison and "relocated." The "priest" of the title is a Kiowa named Tosamah who preaches two sermons -- one on the creative power of "the word," the other on the deicide caused by the Kiowa tribe's loss of the sun dance. (Both of these echo similar concerns and even language in *The Way to Rainy Mountain*). This section also is concerned with Abel's life in Los Angeles, with his girlfriend Milly, whose terrible life has not prevented her learning how to love, and with Martinez, a "bad cop" who gives Abel a savage beating.

Part III ("The Night Chanter") is narrated by Abel's Los Angeles friend, Ben Benally, a Navaho, an absolutely decent person whose healthy attitude toward the world contrasts with the flippancy of Tosamah because he does not pretend to sophisticated intellectual notions and, through the means of the curative powers of the Navaho Night Chant, has maintained his spiritual health.

Part IV ("The Dawn Runner") deals with Abel and his grandfather just after Abel's return to the pueblo. Francisco remembers teaching his grandsons how to understand the seasons in relation to the land, his early hunting and romantic adventures and the "dawn running," which is the tribute of the living to the dead. Then he dies, and Abel runs for him at dawn.

What we see in this sequence is a movement from the dead past of sterility and despair through a present of suffering and hope to the possibility of future health and finally to the eternal wisdom of Francisco and Abel's identification with it. The first stage may be defined ironically in relation to Black Elk's symbolism of the south -- the direction of summer and "the power to grow." This is the power of Francisco, and Part I begins with a description of the agricultural fields of the village and ends with Francisco in his fields, mourning the loss of Abel, whose spiritual ill health may be understood in his alienation both from his grandfather and from the fertility of the fields.

Black Elk associated the west with autumn and with nature's dual powers of creation and destruction, and Abel's experience corresponds to this because in this second stage he is befriended and loved by Milly and almost destroyed by Martinez. Furthermore, the two sermons of Tosamah repeat this same motif of creation and destruction: the creativity of "the word" and the destruction of the Kiowa gods.

Black Elk associated the north and winter with human endurance, and Ben Benally embodies this quality. The passage from the *Night Chant* which is the source of the novel's title and Ben's memories of the beautiful Navaho girl called Pony and of Abel the evening before he returns to the reservation suggest that Ben's strength of character and mind derives from his healthy reconciliation to the earth and that we are to see this stage as one of hope -- and as the thematic antithesis of Part I. And Part IV is clearly the antithesis of Part II because it shows us Francisco's memories of the spiritual "running for the dead" and Abel's running when Francisco dies, running into the "house made of dawn" and, presumably, into the wisdom and understanding which Black Elk associated with spring and with the east.

This reading of the final section of the novel provides little support for Charles R. Larson's claim that Abel returns home to "a kind of ritual suicide" and that his running is toward death (88-89). In fact, the week after Abel's return is itself a reprise of the structure of the novel as I have outlined it. He watches Francisco dying for six days, his actions corresponding to the structure of the first three parts of the novel. On the first two days he gets drunk (Part I); then he has no money, it is cold, and he is sick and in pain (Part II); in despair he listens to Francisco's random words without understanding them (Part III); finally, on the seventh morning, Francisco dies, and Abel prepares the body according to traditional ritual and runs at dawn: "He could see at last without having to think" (191).

James Welch's *Winter in the Blood* also is structured in four parts, and though the author's rather surrealistic methods have filled it with incidents and minor characters its plot is fairly simple and can be easily seen in the terms we have established. Part I deals with the unnamed narrator's return to his mother's farm at a time of drought, his memories of the dead father and brother who were the only people he ever really cared about, his mother's remarriage to an arrogant opportunist, and his encounters with a girl named Marlene and a mysterious tourist whom he calls "the airplane man." In Part II he goes to meet an old Indian named Yellow Calf, who seems to represent the old values and virtues of the tribe but who is to the narrator only a subject of irony and amusement. He loses his chance to be reunited with a former girlfriend, loses Marlene and loses his opportunity to escape to Canada with "the airplane man," who is arrested as a fugitive from the law. In Part III he returns a second time to the farm to find that his traditionalist grandmother has died and to remember the terrible occasion when his brother died. Finally, in Part IV he goes to see Yellow Calf again, discovers that the old man is actually his grandfather, and, as it begins to rain at last, realizes that he finally has begun to achieve understanding.

Clearly Part I, with its subject of ironically perceived life, is balanced with Part III and the death of the narrator's grandmother and brother, while the defeats of Part II are the antithesis of the victory in the coming of wisdom and rain in Part IV. The movement from sterile and meaningless life through defeat and death to final victory and rebirth can therefore be seen as corresponding to the symbolic relationship of the seasons and the directions in Black Elk's vision.

Leslie Marmon Silko's *Ceremony* is not divided conventionally into four sections or even into chapters, but its four-part structure can be seen in spite of the apparent fragmentation of the narrative. The story of Tayo, the Laguna veteran of the war in the Pacific, like that of Abel and Welch's narrator, moves from a first stage of sterility, sickness and drought to wisdom, health and triumph. But the process by which the final triumph is achieved is different, and the plot, particularly in the first stage, mixes the present with the bad memories of the past in a manner which, to a superficial view, may seem jumbled.

Furthermore, the only thing that keeps the narrative's parts from blurring into each other is Silko's use of poems, or, more often, fragments of poems, to divide the prose sections. In all but a few cases the poems are adaptations of Laguna legends, and the most important of these -- and the one which is told in fragments throughout the novel -- is the story of how the people, after losing their plants and animals when they took up Ck'o'yo magic, finally were able to get them back. This story may itself be understood in terms of the structure we have seen in Momaday's novel: (1) for their folly the people are punished with drought, and Hummingbird helps them by creating Fly as a messenger to the Fourth World below this one; (2) in the Fourth World they learn that they must ask Buzzard to purify the town, but Buzzard will not do it without tobacco; (3) they get tobacco from Caterpillar; and (4) Buzzard purifies the town and the Ck'o'yo magic is driven out.

This story, supplemented by others in the poems, accompanies Silko's story of the sickness of Tayo, the curing ceremony which is the beginning of his redemption, his discovery of the powers of nature, and his final victory over "the witchery." At the risk of appearing arbitrary, I suggest that the first stage in Tayo's story, corresponding to the first sections of the novels by Momaday and Welch, is that which deals with his bad memories -- of the war, his cousin Rocky's death, his experience in the veterans' psychiatric hospital, his mother's death, and his fight with the murderous veteran Emo -- during the day that ends when he is finally able to sleep "without dreams" (105). Significantly, this section reveals the greatest complexity of plot, because for Tayo the past and the present are virtually indistinguishable, and his mental ill health may be understood as the crippling of the present by the past.

Except for a frightening memory of living as a small child with his mother in the hobo jungle in Gallup, the second stage in Tayo's journey to wisdom and health is chronological. It deals with his encounter with the Navaho medicine man Betonie, who performs for him a curing ceremony, which he says is incomplete, and his return home to further drunkenness, to an encounter with the pathetic Ute girl Helen Jean, and to "trying to vomit out everything -- all the past, all his life" (168). The incompleteness of Betonie's ceremony must be emphasized, because it might appear that the structure of Tayo's journey from sickness to health is different from what we have seen. In the second sections of *House Made of Dawn* and *Winter in the Blood* the effects are negative: Abel's "relocation" and the various defeats of Welch's narrator. Tayo goes through the curing ceremony, but it cannot save him until the wisdom he has received from Betonie has been seasoned by later events.

The third stage is linked to the second by the poem about Kaup'a'ta, who gambled with the people, won their lives and stole the rain-bringing clouds, and about the Sun, who learned from his spider grandmother how to trick the Gambler, win back the clouds and restore the people to life. In this stage Tayo searches for the cattle that his uncle Josiah lost, escapes death at the hands of cowboys who think he is a cattle thief, and meets the mysterious woman Ts'eh, who teaches him the wisdom which can be learned from nature.

The final and briefest stage begins with Tayo's return from the mountains and the discovery that all the stories he has heard are his own story, that he is not insane after all, and that he can escape the "witchery" only if he does not succumb to the temptation to fight the world with its own murderous weapons.

The similarities in the structures of the three novels and their relation to the structure of Black Elk's definition of the symbolism of the four directions and seasons can be seen when we reduce them to essentials:

I   (Black Elk's south and summer, "the power to grow"):
    Momaday -- Abel's sterility and self-hatred; the murder of the albino.
    Welch -- the narrator's sterility; drought.
    Silko -- loss of plants and animals to Ck'o'yo magic; Tayo's illness;
    drought.

II (Black Elk's west, autumn, creation and destruction):
Momaday -- Abel's physical suffering; Milly's love.
Welch -- defeat of narrator's hopes and meeting Yellow Calf without recognition.
Silko -- Hummingbird and Fly's descent into the Fourth World; Betonie's curing ceremony.

III (Black Elk's north, winter, human endurance):
Momaday -- Ben Benally; the Night Chant.
Welch -- death of narrator's grandmother and memory of his brother's death.
Silko -- Caterpillar's gift of the necessary tobacco; Tayo's life with Ts'eh in the natural world.

IV (Black Elk's east, spring, wisdom and understanding):
Momaday -- Abel's running for his grandfather.
Welch -- narrator's recognition that Yellow Calf is his grandfather; end of drought.
Silko -- Buzzard's purification of the town; Tayo's escape from "witchery."

In writing *Ceremony* Silko presumably was influenced at least to a degree by Momaday's novel, and Welch has credited both Momaday and Silko as influences (Coltelli 198). But we need not assume that the structural similarities of the three novels are a matter either of influence or coincidence. Nor need we assume that the structure was derived directly from Black Elk. But we must assume that all three originate in a common perception, derived from a wisdom that lies deep in the American Indian consciousness, of protagonists who are ill because they cannot relate to their world and who must pass through three stages to reach a fourth stage of wisdom. Obviously the parallels are inexact -- the novels would be of little value if they were only copies of each other -- but their common structure derives from a vision that originates in the shared Indian experience of their authors. Any attempt to define an American Indian literary tradition must take account of that vision.

CHAPTER V

AMERICAN INDIAN POETRY AS CULTURAL MEDIATION

The first point to be made about the virtual explosion of poetry by the present generation of poets identified as American Indians is that the phenomenon derives much of its importance and the poetry itself draws much of its strength from factors which are universally to be found in the process by which a colonial literature evolves into a national literature. When we examine the earliest effort in any former colony to define a national literature -- including that of American writers in the earliest years of the republic -- we find an inevitable tension between, on the one hand, a powerful assertion of belief in the new nation's cultural uniqueness and, on the other, an unavoidable influence of the literature of the colonizing nation and even an allegiance to it. Americans who wrote poetry and fiction in the thirty years after the Revolution could not ignore the eighteenth century English models which they had read when they still considered themselves Englishmen, but they aspired to the ideal of an American literature that would be different from and greater than its parent. In *The Sketch Book*, therefore, Washington Irving paid homage to the "mother country" while declaring independence from her, and the book expresses his combination of a willingness to emulate English literary models with claims for King Philip and the Dutchmen of the Hudson Valley as legitimate literary subjects.

This development of a national American literature out of traditions well-established during almost two colonial centuries may seem irrelevant to our understanding of the nation-building we have observed in Asia and Africa in the last half of this century. After all, the colonials who considered themselves Americans in the eighteenth century also thought of themselves, at least until 1776, as Englishmen in every detail except that of residence. These Anglo-Americans could assert their uniqueness as a people to justify their political independence, but in fact before independence and even after it for a time they were still Englishmen in culture, and writers of the early republic understood their task as one of proving that they were something else.

What distinguishes this experience from that of new African nations is the fact that a Nigerian writer, for example, knows that when his country was a British colony Nigerians were not Englishmen. The intelligentsia in place at the time of independence was a product of a school system modeled upon British example, and many of its members had learned about government and, probably what was more important to them, had learned about bureaucracy in a British civil service and in British universities. But race defined the difference. The population of Nigeria and the population of the United Kingdom were eternally divided from the beginning.

And yet Nigeria's writers before and after independence wrote in English and understood what they were doing in the light of the British writers they had read in school. (Consider, for example, the influence of Yeats and Eliot reflected in two of Chinua Achebe's titles -- *Things Fall Apart* and *No Longer At Ease*.) This combination of cultural allegiance to a venerable literary tradition with awareness of a responsibility for formulating a literary definition of nationality produces much of the tension in Nigerian writing, and it may be compared to the circumstances in which so many contemporary American Indian poets find themselves.

When writers seek to define themselves either racially *or* culturally as American Indians, their relationship both to that context and to the larger American context of which they are inevitably a part resembles the colonial literary predicament we have described. Indian poets must derive what they need from the larger surrounding culture, but they must not seem to be only a part of that culture. They also must establish themselves as Indian writers even though most of their audience is not Indian.

This predicament may be likened to that in which white South African writers find themselves. South African society may be compared to that of Britain's former American colonies in the early nineteenth century because of its English-speaking component, but it is unlike the early American republic not only because of its enormous African population, which is much larger than either the slave or Indian population of the United States in that period, but also because of the Afrikaners, its "white tribe." The predicament of South Africa's white writers, both in English and in Afrikaans, can be understood in terms of three strategies. One is that of Afrikaans poets, who inevitably must write for a small audience. (Breyten Breytenbach has achieved an international audience because of the special political notoriety of his case. No other Afrikaans poet has achieved a comparable reputation abroad.) Afrikaans novelists also will write for a small audience unless they can achieve translation abroad. (The strategy of Andre Brink, for example, has been to publish Afrikaans editions in South Africa and then to prepare his own translations for publication in Britain and America.) And writers in English -- Nadine Gordimer, for example -- may seek to achieve critical and commercial success in the English-speaking world, even if that means, to a degree, skewing the writing to a foreign rather than a domestic audience.

The predicament of American Indians writing poetry in Lakota or Cherokee, if there are any, is precisely that of the Afrikaans poets of South Africa. If they were to write in tribal languages and translate their work into English for publication, they would escape their predicament as Andre Brink has escaped his. But the great majority of American Indian poets find themselves in the predicament in which Nadine Gordimer found herself at the beginning of her career when she presumably realized that her real audience was in Britain and the United States, and they pursue their own version of her strategy, by writing in the language of the dominant culture and finding almost all of their audience in that culture. American Indian poetry, in other words, is Indian, but, more than that, it is American.

Having said that, we next must consider the question of the extent to which American Indian poets are indebted to the tribal cultures from which they derive. As we have seen, the tribal designations which characteristically follow the names of Indian writers in parentheses do not necessarily indicate anything more than racial background, even when they are "pure" rather than oddly mixed, as in, for example, the Chemehuevi-Chippewa poet Diane Burns. As for indebtedness to tribal culture, poets who have been identified as American Indian, as we suggested in Chapter I, may be understood according to their position in a wide spectrum. Simon Ortiz (Acoma) and Lucy Tapahonso (Navaho) and even Harold Littlebird, the son of parents from *two* pueblo tribes (Laguna and Santo Domingo), are obviously rooted in tribal traditions. At the other extreme we see Diane Glancy (Cherokee) and Jim Barnes ("Welsh-Choctaw"). Both have claimed for themselves tribal identities which are hardly based on experience, and they could be considered white writers if they wanted it that way. Between these two extremes we find much complexity. On the one hand, there are writers who were brought up by parents or grandparents or other family members who imbued in them a thorough sense of tribal identity, even though they were to a degree removed from the tribe itself. Duane Niatum is an example. Powerfully influenced in childhood and adolescence by a Klallam grandfather and great-uncle, he is a Klallam in ways that have nothing to do with race or residence on a reservation. On the other hand there are those poets who were separated from a tribal life in childhood or even at birth and have sought to develop a tribal sense through study and will-power.

In this latter category we find some of the most distinguished American Indian poets. As we have seen, Wendy Rose, though she has done little with her Miwok origins but guess at them and though her Hopi descent is patrilineal and thus insignificant as far as the Hopis are concerned, has studied Hopi culture thoroughly as an anthropologist and has not only appropriated a Hopi identity but also has come to terms with her British and German ancestors by an equally powerful act of imagination. Linda Hogan derives on the side of one parent from Oklahoma Chickasaws, but she grew up in Colorado, and by study and above all by writing poems she has discovered the significance of her racial identity -- which includes a consciousness of descent both from a great Chickasaw chief and from a white pioneer who homesteaded in Nebraska. As she told Joseph Bruchac in an interview, "the split between the two cultures in my life became a growing abyss and [poems] were what I did to heal it" (*Survival* 122).

Perhaps a more special case is that of Maurice Kenny, who was exiled from his Mohawk reservation by disorientations in his family. And yet though he has been cut off at least to a degree from his origins, he presents a remarkable example of a poet who best understands the value of what he has lost *because* he has lost it. An early poem, "Going Home," is almost too painful to read in its account of a bus ride back to the reservation in the depths of a bad winter:

> ... it was a long ride ...
> home from Brooklyn to the reservation
> that was not home
> to songs I could not sing
> to dances I could not dance ...
> home to a Nation, Mohawk
> to faces I did not know
> and hands which did not recognize me
> to names and doors
> my father shut (*Between Two Rivers*, p. 44)

And yet Kenny, through a powerful act of the imagination, knows what it means to be a Mohawk. His poem "Wild Strawberry" (*Between Two Rivers* 55) is an example of the way he has discovered his Mohawk origins by realizing to what degree he cannot recover them. It was apparently inspired by another winter bus ride, in this case from the reservation back to Brooklyn, to eat not very good strawberries imported from Mexico and to remember from childhood a spring-time experience of picking wild strawberries on the reservation. The significance of this memory, as he wrote with particular reference to this poem in one of the autobiographical essays in the Swann-Krupat collection, is in the traditional symbolism of the strawberry: "The wild strawberry ... is the symbol of life to the Iroquois people" (47). Most of his poem describes his memory of a particular Mohawk strawberry-picking experience, a memory and a meaning enhanced by his exile from that experience, as we see in the poem's last four lines:

> I sit here in Brooklyn eating Mexican
> berries which I did not pick, nor do
> I know the hands which did, nor their stories ...
> January snow falls, listen ... (*Between Two Rivers* 56).

In the previous chapter I discussed four prose works in the light of what I suggested as an American Indian literary tradition. In that light it is worth wondering what Indian poets, judging by what they say about influences on their work, assume to be their tradition. This is a much more complex question. In the present cosmopolitan era no Indian novelist, even one thoroughly conditioned by tribal experience, can be free of influence by a wide range of literary examples, including that of Indian predecessors. As we have seen, Welch has cited both Momaday and Silko as influences. But he also cites as masters Steinbeck, Hemingway (for his "vivid economical style"), and, presumably in translation, the Italian novelist Elio Vittorini, for *In Sicily* (Coltelli 193, 198). And Momaday frequently has acknowledged the influence of Faulkner, particularly "The Bear." No American novel, regardless of its author's race or cultural heritage, can stand in isolation from the wide range of work produced in America and Europe in the last two hundred years.

That also is, and at the same time is not, the case with a poem. Its eclectic origins may be equally or even more complex and wide-ranging, but its concentration and brevity may obscure our usual sense of what we mean by "influence." Shakespeare and the English Romantics have been mentioned by more than one Indian poet as a personal inspiration, as have Whitman, Dickinson, and a wide range of Indian and non-Indian American poets of the present generation and that immediately previous to it. But they also have mentioned various Latin American and Chinese poets and Japanese writers of haiku.

Given this wide-ranging eclecticism it is often dismaying to read what Indian poets say about the forces that have shaped their literary consciousness. I am not referring to simple racist hooey like Jimmie Durham's literary equivalent of frothing at the mouth: "I absolutely hate this country. Not just the government, but the culture, the group of people called Americans. The country. I hate the country. I HATE AMERICA" (Swann and Krupat 163). Speaking for myself, such babbling gives me no desire to read Durham's poems and makes me suspect that they may well be fatally crippled by the political fanaticism which apparently inspired his outburst. (In contrast, Duane Niatum's remark that "[Didacticism] goes against my aesthetic ..." [Bruchac, *Survival* 205] is cool and recognizably human.)

I also am not referring to merely silly remarks like that of Joy Harjo when she was asked in an interview why "Anglos" travel so much: "Oh, it's because ... they're always moving to get away from their mothers" (Bruchac, *Survival* 93).

Of course, we must not be too harsh on things said in interviews when everything is off the cuff and cannot be adequately considered. But one suspects that when Paula Gunn Allen, for example, erupts into the following outburst of mere rant her mind is untroubled by anything resembling a fact:

> ... the Western world. ... All it can do is produce death and contemplate death and think about death. ... And that's why I call them the death culture. They're obsessed with dying. ... You know, Westerners have died at a greater rate in the past five hundred years than anyone else. You know that. You know what the population of Europe was in 1495 or 1750 (Coltelli 30).

To this I can only say that though I cannot claim to possess exact knowledge of the extent of Europe's population in 1495 and 1750 I know enough about it to be sure that if Allen thinks there were more people in Europe two hundred or five hundred years ago than there are today she just doesn't know what she's talking about.

Of course, as we have seen -- in Chapter II -- Allen's grasp of historical detail is hardly her greatest strength. For example, in the same interview she said that "in this country there are over a million non-Indians to every Indian" and then to show that these wild numbers are not due to bad editing she repeated them on the next page only to refer four pages later to "a million Indians in this country" [Coltelli 13, 14, 18-19]. Whatever we say about this it is clear that when all of Allen's numbers are put together she is either saying that there are only 250 American Indians or she is saying that there are a trillion people in the United States.

But leaving aside the carelessness of these remarks, what is most depressing about them is that they are uttered in the context of Allen's claims of Mozart and Charlotte Bronte and William Carlos Williams and Keats and Shelley, among many others, as influences on her life and work (Coltelli 37). "Western" culture is obsessed with death, but it has given life to Paula Gunn Allen.

When Indian poets speak of a tradition they invariably refer to concerns which in our culture are usually assumed to be traditionally Indian -- a vital relationship to the natural world and a sense of community and of tribal place in the land. The latter is assumed the case even by poets who are unclear about their own relationship to a tribe and have no reservation experience. They usually imply that their tribal origins and in particular the oral traditions of the tribe are more important in their understanding of the literary traditions in which they work than anything derived from the "Euro-American" culture which they have studied in colleges or universities. But in spite of these tribal concerns many do not know a tribal language, though some have made claims for the language of their tribal ancestors at the expense of what is in fact their native language -- English. Joy Harjo, for example, said in a 1982 interview that it was not easy for her "to say things well" in English because she considered the language "very materialistic and ... very subject-oriented" compared to Creek, of which she admitted she knew nothing but a few words (Bruchac, *Survival* 94). The thrust of this remark is that the language of Shakespeare and Keats and Whitman and Dickinson, to say nothing of the King

James Bible, is not really very "spiritual" and is much more egotistic and less community-oriented (and, of course, much more "male-dominated") than a language about which Harjo doesn't really know very much, and it is to her credit that only three years later she was embarrassed enough to say of English that "I have learned to love the language [and] what the language can express" (Coltelli 62). The faults of English, in other words, are not in the language but in its mis-use by shysters and fools. Its most obvious vindication is in the example of the language's greatest poets, and Harjo's difficulty in writing in it not only is belied by her own substantial artistic success but finally can be seen to be nothing more than the difficulty that all of us encounter when we write.

In other words, the first thing to say about an American Indian poetic tradition is that Indian poets write in English. They are products of a mixed culture because of that primary fact. And most of them have acquired their literary education in university English departments. Even if they know a tribal language, even if like Lance Henson and Lucy Tapahonso they use Cheyenne or Navaho words or even sentences in their English texts, their work is derived in great part from an American literary tradition.

In this connection it is worth saying that, as we have seen, those writers who are most secure in their tribal identity may find the least difficulty in relating to a cosmopolitan cultural tradition. For one example, Duane Niatum, whose sense of himself as a Klallam is apparently profound and secure, has been inspired by his reading of the journals and letters of Impressionist and Post-impressionist European painters to write poems which pay homage to that great artistic tradition, and his indebtedness to his education at the University of Washington is so heartfelt that he has written a series of poems in homage to Theodore Roethke, his master -- four of them (the magic Indian number, notice) and sonnets at that. His "Lines for Roethke Twenty Years After His Death" (in his own *Harper's Anthology*, pp. 103-105) not only obey the traditional sonnet's requirements in meter and rhyme but they echo, without imitating, the cadence and rhythmic quality that characterizes the poems of

Roethke's last phase, and their diction, in no sense copied from those poems, somehow sounds like Roethke's.

Of course, Niatum may seem out of the mainstream of contemporary Indian poetry in his apparent classicism. The tradition in which he works is not that which begins in Whitman, culminates in the "Beats," and inspires a majority of contemporary Indian poets. His tradition begins in the English Metaphysicals, it enters the twentieth century by way of Eliot's theory and practice, it reaches its apogee in the premises of the New Criticism, the achievement of Roethke and Louise Bogan -- both of them Niatum's personal acquaintances -- and also the Robert Lowell of *Lord Weary's Castle*, and, as he has said, it was fortified by his reading of "the real poets" -- Hardy, Auden, Yeats, Stevens, "to name a few" -- to whose work he was directed by his professors (Swann and Krupat 132).

When talking about the origins of their muse, all American poets make most sense when they recognize the inter-relationship of their local tradition (be it racial, cultural, regional, religious, or whatever) to the larger American tradition of which it is a part. Indian poets are American in this sense. Simon Ortiz seemed to suggest an even broader awareness when he said in an interview, "I write about universal things. What else could I write about? I write about the same things that Robert Browning or Shelley or Shakespeare did ..." (Coltelli 116) And Niatum has said that the "sources that helped me grow were Roethke and his literary fathers and mothers [who] taught me the ways of art, and my great-uncle and grandfather [who taught me] the ways of nature" (Swann and Krupat 135-136), and he has indicated his awareness of the universality of the best aspects of these two traditions when he said that Roethke's poems "reflect the Native American tradition" in their awareness of our "relationship to nature" (Bruchac, *Survival* 208).

And if it is true that Indian poets cannot be understood in isolation from the larger American culture of which they are a part, it is also true that American culture depends for its ultimate meaning on an understanding of its Indian elements. N. Scott Momaday has claimed for the American Indian a primary place not only in major works of American literature but in "the American imagination":

> The American Indian is indispensable to the soil and the dream and the destiny of America. ... He always will be a central figure in the American imagination, a central figure in American literature. We can't very well do without him (Bruchac, *Survival* 189).

If Momaday is right -- and I for one am certain that he is -- that American culture is eternally indebted to the Indian, then the other side of this truth is that American Indian literature and the literature of the rest of our culture are so inter-related that they cannot be separated. As I have said, the primary fact about American Indian poets is that they are American poets. They are like the grandchildren of Norwegian or Irish immigrants who are thoroughly Americanized but somehow feel themselves more Norwegian or Irish than their parents even though they cannot speak their grandparents' Norse or Gaelic. As a "Native American" an Indian might not realize this and may even deny it, but how else may we understand the experience of an Indian whose parents or grandparents have moved to the city -- colonials in a new urban world in the same essential circumstances as those of nineteenth century Norwegian immigrants when they chose to leave their mountains for the Dakota prairie?

We can avoid many errors if we remember that a poem by an Indian poet should be judged by the only legitimate test of any poem. Does it speak to our universal condition? If it does not, its social and political value will not matter.

It is worth considering Adrian C. Louis in this light. His poems reveal a remarkable degree of contemporary sophistication in their presentation in gritty images of the social reality of the grim place that Pine Ridge, the Oglala Sioux reservation in South Dakota, apparently has become. Pine Ridge's county is perhaps the poorest in the country, but Louis, a brave writer who seems unafflicted with any illusions about anything at all, knows that what ails the place cannot be so easily explained. Because the reservation is legally "dry," a tiny settlement called White Clay, just below the Nebraska line a few miles south of the town of Pine Ridge, prospers on its enormous trade with Indians who go there to spend their welfare checks on booze, drink themselves insensible, and too often kill themselves driving home. Even worse than that is the degree of domestic abuse described in some of the most horrific episodes in Louis's one novel, *Skins* (1995).

What saves his subject from being only social, what makes it universally human and yet specific to the reality of Pine Ridge, is that Louis balances his sardonic and even brutal portrait of the frightful reality of the reservation with a profound sense of loss and the sad knowledge that traditional tribal values have been forgotten by so many Oglalas. One poem in *Vortex of Indian Fevers* (1995), "Looking for Judas," describes an illegally killed deer hanging gutted in the moonlight. The speaker senses that the deer deserves religious awe and also that he himself is the Judas without whom the religious implications of the experience cannot be understood. The poem's last lines lead to a sardonic conclusion that exactly defines the tragic break with traditional tribal wisdom:

> They say before the white man
> brought us Jesus, we had honor.
> They say when we killed the Deer People,
> we told them their spirits
> would live in our flesh.
> We used bows of ash, no spotlights, no rifles,
> and their holy blood became ours.
> Or something like that.

The final line is not meant for those committed to sentimentality about Indians revering "Mother Earth" more than the rest of us do. Louis knows that if some Indians do so too many others don't, and his vision forces us to face a darker truth -- that the Indianness of that reverence does not mean that every Indian possesses it, that the accident of being born Indian does not necessarily make anyone any saintlier than anyone else, that the wisdom of Black Elk or any other holy man is not inherited in the blood but embraced in the heart, and that even Indians can be brutal not only toward the environment but toward each other.

His success in achieving this balance of anger and wisdom may seem remarkable, considering the fact that he is not an Oglala at all -- or perhaps that fact explains it. His ancestry is Paiute and apparently also white, and he grew up in Nevada, took two degrees at Brown University, and has known Pine Ridge only since 1984, when he began teaching there.

Whatever the source of his strengths, however, the poems they make possible are more than local in their significance. The betrayal of ideals for the sake of foolish and ephemeral goals is a basic human fault, and those of us who know this will read Louis with a shock of recognition which is both disturbing and necessary.

As an outsider at Pine Ridge, Louis writes poems that are more Indian in general than tribally Oglala in particular. Can a specifically tribal vision, no matter how small or remote the tribe, be seen as an expression of universal awareness?

Lance Henson is a Southern Cheyenne who was brought up in Oklahoma by grandparents to whom the traditions and culture of their tribe were a living presence, and his own allegiance to the teachings of the Native American Church and his membership in the Cheyenne Dog Soldier Society are inevitable results of that upbringing. From the beginning of his career as a poet he has adhered to the most exacting minimalist standards, writing poems that are brief, enigmatic, and almost totally dependent on their images, and he makes no compromise with the reader's unwillingness to read them slowly with full attention to the symbolic resonance of the words. A Henson poem depends for its success on his ability to produce images that carry its emotional burden and thus its meaning. Clearly Henson's methods suggest that he has been influenced by the Oriental poets mentioned in several of his poems, and he has expressed an indebtedness to American and Latin American surrealists, but the primary origins of his poetic vision are in two larger traditions which reflect the inter-relationship of American Indian and European elements.

For one thing, his ability to define a spiritual or emotional state in terms of one small, sharply delineated physical place is clearly within the traditions of American Indian thought. When Black Elk defined his vision in terms of the symbolism of the four directions he was saying that by definition the earth itself was the ultimate symbol of all spiritual reality. In other words, if we are wise, we see meaning wherever we look, and Henson's remark to Bruchac in an interview that "everybody's home should be the center of the world" (*Survival* 108) reminds us of Black Elk's remark to Neihardt that "anywhere is the center of the world."

At the same time this assumption that even the smallest manifestation of the world of nature may be a symbol of a profound spiritual truth resembles a venerable notion in the New England tradition which goes back not only to the Transcendentalists but to the Puritanism which is one of Emerson's philosophical roots and which is expressed early in our literature in Jonathan Edwards' catalogue of "Images and Shadows of Divine Things."

It also should be said that Henson's conception of the "small" poem and his allegiance to his tribe's warrior traditions are appropriate to a poet so deeply conscious of his tribal identity. The Cheyennes were a relatively small tribe whose warriors were able, through great courage and a passionate loyalty to their people, to put off to the last their conquest by an enemy who finally overwhelmed them through mere strength of numbers and superior firepower. As a Marine veteran, a student of the martial arts, and a descendant of warriors who were among the bravest and noblest soldiers America has ever produced, Henson is profoundly conscious of the military ideal, and he has achieved a harmonious balance in his own vision of the poet and the Cheyenne warrior he rightly believes himself to be.

At the same time these American Indian perceptions are expressed within the context of a conception of language which is Platonic. "We are born out of a perfect state to be here," he told Bruchac. "I think brevity is ... one way to acknowledge and pay homage to the Great Silence we came out of" (*Survival* 114). In other words, it is language which links the imperfection in which we have our physical being to the perfection from which we spiritually derive, a magic which can only be dissipated in a long poem. The great white space around a Henson poem therefore is the silence in which words (as echoes of the Word, the *Logos*) most effectively sound and in which the images that words make possible most powerfully resonate with meanings beyond themselves.

Henson's method, therefore, is to create striking images related to the history and wisdom of his Cheyenne forbears, receiving power from those traditions while insuring their survival by enriching them in a kind of symbiosis of the traditional and the personal which is often wonderful to behold.

One of the most remarkable aspects of Henson's career as a poet is the fact that though he is deeply rooted in the Oklahoma soil that gave him birth he is widely traveled, reading his work and offering poetry workshops in over five hundred educational institutions and acquiring a network of admirers and translators in Europe. Indeed his subject in his later work often has been his own European experience, and those poems are significant attempts to bridge the gulf between European culture and his own Cheyenne origins, a transatlantic leap which often produces remarkable effects -- as in the Cheyenne words sprinkled in German translations in *Poems for a master beadworker* (1993).

Henson knows that America is largely a country of immigrants and that he not only finds his native land by leaving it -- the usual experience of the American writer abroad -- but is able to perceive Europe most clearly because he is, in a sense, an immigrant himself -- in Europe.

This is not to say that he is under any illusion that Europe is an appropriate alternative to America. The images in his poems with European settings are often ominous. In "walking at teutoberger wald," for example, the peaceful scene is contrasted with the forest's losses to acid rain:

> it is a war zone here
> like everywhere
> mother earths damp and darkened skin
> weeping for us all
> for us all (*Another Distance* 29).

What this poem demonstrates is that Henson's use of allusion is not only tribal but cosmopolitan. Its power is enhanced by the fact (only implied) that the Teutoberg Forest is the setting of the victory in 9 A.D. of the German tribesmen of Arminius over the Roman legions. Whatever judgment is made of that victory, or of Custer's over the Cheyennes on the Washita, the old victories and defeats seem less important than the present predicament -- basic, environmental, international -- of the entire race in a world which continues to be threatened by social and biological stupidity. Henson clearly is energized by a belief that for that stupidity the only corrective is the wisdom inherent in a tribal vision, translated into awareness of our universal condition.

Nowhere in Henson's work is his faith in the value and universal significance of the vision of his tribe more movingly demonstrated than in "we are a people," a poem with a title which is in fact to be understood as its first line.

> we are a people
>
> days pass easy over these ancient hills
>
> i wander near a moccasin path overgrown with
> rusted cans and weeds
> i stand in the forest at sunset waiting for
> a song from the rising wind
>
> it is this way forever in this place
> there is no distance between the name
> of my race
> and the owl calling
> nor the badgers gentle
> plodding
>
> we are a people born under symbols
> that rise from the dust to touch us
> that pass through the cedars where
> our old ones sleep
>
> to tell us of their dreams (*Selected Poems* 20)

Henson's success in this poem in capturing the sense of the vital relationship of the present to the past, of the individual to the tribe, and of the individual and the tribe to the natural world is all the more miraculous considering the fact that he has done all of this with so few materials. The key to our understanding of it is in the statement that "the name / of my race" is one with the sound of the owl's call and the "gentle plodding" of the badger, which, given the fact that Henson identifies with badgers because his Cheyenne name means "Badger," is also his own sound. When we add to this the fact that the Cheyenne name for themselves is *tsis tsis tas*, meaning "the people," the title of the poem "we are a people" means not only "we *really are* a people" but also "we are Cheyennes." To be a Cheyenne, in other words, is to be aware of the lack of "distance" between the Cheyennes and the sound of the owl and the badger and the poet himself. The final statement, "we are a people born under symbols," therefore, means that to be a Cheyenne is to live in a vital relationship to a vast complex of symbolism that rises out of the very dust of the natural world and from the graves of the ancestors who are present in the dust, in the sounds of nature, and in the dreams they communicate to their descendants. The "ancient hills," the forest, the sound of the wind, the sense of eternity, the Cheyennes in their graves and in the poet's consciousness, the owl and the badger, earth and spirit, past and present, the poet and his people -- all are vitally related to one another, indeed are metaphors for one another, in this extraordinary moment of perception.

Needless to say, a poet deeply rooted in a tribal tradition runs the risk of losing those readers who may think they encounter too many difficulties in relating to the Cheyenne elements in his poems. But when Bruchac asked him how he thought a reader who did not know Cheyenne culture could relate to his poems, Henson said, "I think the Cheyenne way is a model for people looking at 'tribes' and how they operate" (*Survival* 109). The significance of this answer is greater than Henson probably intended: all human experience, in a sense, is tribal, and all of us are members of a tribe, whether we know it or not. All of us, that is, are able to look at the world only in relation to the vision we have received from our culture. Obviously our universal humanity is by definition what we share with all people everywhere, but we see those people from our own more or less narrow perspective. In light of this, a tribal art as overt as Henson's may enable us to see both the limitations of our own tribal vision *and* our common humanity with members of other tribes. All of us, at least in our best moments, are "waiting for / a song from the rising wind," standing in the present, struggling to relate to the past and to our ancestors, living in a natural world to which we know we must relate; and none of us can be saved, or can save ourselves, except by the liberating power of language. The symbols "rise from the dust to touch us," and when we are not foolish we know that this is true.

In an autobiographical essay Simon Ortiz makes precisely this point: "It is language that brings us into being in order to know life" (Swann and Krupat 187). This essay, in fact, is a hymn of praise to the very phenomenon of language, and Ortiz knows that language is so important, every language, that his own acquisition of English as a second language enriched him, even as it was accompanied by the pain of attending a government school on the Acoma Reservation where children were punished if they spoke their mother tongue. Ortiz knows that when his parents and grandparents told him to "educate yourself in order to help your people" (Swann and Krupat 191), they meant, even if they did not say so, that any addition to the language of the people of Acoma was of benefit to all of them.

As we have seen, the great majority of the poets we have described are conscious of standing with a foot in each of two cultures, and the dual nature of their stance derives not only from experience of the total American culture but from consciousness of mixed racial inheritance. Any definition of an American Indian poetic tradition must take account of this dualism and of the fact that many Indian poets perceive their function both in their tribes and in the larger culture of America as one of mediation between an Indian vision, whether tribal or "pan-Indian," and the dominant culture surrounding it.

This dual awareness may be a heavy burden. Joy Harjo's description of her sense of herself as a "mixed blood" is painful:

> I walk in and out of many worlds. I used to see being born of this
> mixed-blood / mixed vision a curse, and hated myself for it. It was
> too confusing and destructive when I saw the world through that
> focus. The only message I got was not belonging anywhere, not to
> any side. I have since decided that being familiar with more than one
> world, more than one vision, is a blessing, and I know I make my
> own choices. I also know that it is only an illusion that any of the
> worlds are separate (Swann and Krupat 266).

The "half-breed" consciousness, in other words, is a burden, but it also is a source of

strength and wisdom, indeed a kind of blessing. As Harjo said in an interview, "you

have to believe that you're special to be born like that because ... with it came some

special kind of vision to help you get through it all and to help others through it

because in a way you do see two sides but also see there are more than two sides"

(Bruchac, *Survival* 95).

Wendy Rose, who has said that one of her favorite subjects in pictorial art is

the centaur because it reflects her own "hybrid status ... misunderstood and isolated

-- whether with Indians or with non-Indians" (Coltelli 121), also has said that the

"half-breed" phenomenon is a metaphor for divisions in all of us: "We are in fact all

half-breed in this world today" (Coltelli 123). Paula Gunn Allen has referred to "a

mediational capacity that is not possessed by either of the sides" (Bruchac, *Survival*

19). Joseph Bruchac has referred to a Lakota word for "Translator's Son," which

"means that you are able to understand the language of both sides, to help them

understand each other" (Swann and Krupat 203). As Harjo has said, "We're all in

this together. It's a realization I came to after dealing with the whole half-breed

question. I realized that I'm not separate from myself either, and neither are Indian

people separate from the rest of the world" (Bruchac, *Survival* 96).

These statements seem sane and civilized when compared to most claims of

those who argue that Indian cultures are unique and share no common ground with

other cultures. For an example, consider Thomas E. Sanders, who claims descent

from the Nippawanock tribe of New England but also says he is Cherokee and who, in a moment of self-labelling, called himself, at least in 1973, "Prince Nippawanock." In an article which begins with a reference to the "genocidal intent of the Transplant American in the western hemisphere" (256), he provides a catalogue of pompous generalizations about the moral, social, political, religious, cultural, artistic and miscellaneous shortcomings of the "Transplants." It requires a considerable impudence, even in a "prince," to dismiss an entire civilization. If the word *Transplant* means anything it implies that the "planting" in the American earth of Americans of European descent is artificial and that Indians somehow by being Indians are more deeply rooted in America than anyone else. But what gives Sanders, some of whose ancestors, by the way, were Europeans, the right to impose such arrogant posturing on his readers? And what does it contribute to a wider understanding of the complex business of being an American?

The truth of the matter is that the American Indian poet, who is probably of mixed racial heritage and in any case will be conscious of derivation from a hybrid culture, actually is blessed with a particular angle of vision. But that vision is valuable not because it provides a variety of poseurs with an excuse for keeping groups irreconcilably divided but because it makes possible a perception of the need for the reconciliation of the conflicting elements of the American psyche. When Bruchac mentioned to Linda Hogan the view of Indian traditionalists that "we have a physical part, a mental part, and a spiritual part and it is important to keep them in balance" (*Survival* 130), she agreed:

> Any kind of racism at this point is not good for any people. ... Talk about a balance of things -- talk about head and heart or head and soul -- somehow I think that merging the two cultures ... might be an integration in [that] way.... Indians have already begun that process. Years ago. Now I see white people integrating in that way (132).

I am certain that it is this awareness that caused Simon Ortiz, in his preface to *From Sand Creek* (1981), to say, "I hope, finally, we will all learn something from each other. We must. We are all with and within each other" (7).

I know of no more hopeful sign that a new understanding of American consciousness is possible, a syncretic vision which takes account of all the hitherto divided elements of the American psyche -- Indian and landscape, European and African -- than the fact that Ortiz, himself so fully Indian, and, more precisely, so fully a product of the pueblo of Acoma, should be capable of so wise a vision of the larger American identity. His example suggests that if we learn to rise above the superficialities of race when we define the elements of our culture, if we learn, that is, to understand not only our Indian writers but the larger literary culture of which they are so vital a part as expressions of the essential unity of the diverse elements of American experience, we finally may resolve the old question of what the term *American* means and indeed may begin to realize our old dream of becoming brothers and sisters at last.

CHAPTER VI

AMERICAN MYTH, OLD AND NEW

Myth holds a people together and gives them purpose and direction. It is tempting to say, therefore, given our social and cultural fragmentation, that Americans may be a people without a myth. But the truth is that for more than two hundred years we have had a myth which is associated with the ideals of democracy, freedom, and in particular freedom of economic enterprise, a myth which informs, and is informed by, what has been called our civil religion. That civil religion may or may not any longer possess force, intellectuals may think there is no such myth, and social critics may say that if there is such a thing we have not lived up to it. But if this is so we must explain just what our cultural spokesmen mean when they constantly refer to "the American dream" and why it has been possible for civil rights to be enhanced in the second half of the twentieth century. Surely a minority could not have achieved school desegregation and equality at the polls without reminding the majority of its mythical beliefs.

But if that is the American myth, then somewhere between that myth and our historical record lies legend, which resembles the record in its cast of characters but also resembles the myth in originating in the aspirations rather than in the intellectual courage of the public. The cast of legendary characters includes names both famous and less known, but it also includes symbolic figures, cardboard cut-outs sometimes erected to prove something or other or merely to be knocked down. One of them, the "vanishing American," was simultaneously convenient both to the moral concerns and to the racist assumptions of white America. Two others, the "red devil" who interfered savagely with the progress of the pioneers and the "blood brother" who preferred peace to war, inform Cooper's fictional division of an entire race into "good" and "bad" Indians, stereotypes still with us today in the film "Dances With Wolves," in which the saintly Sioux are idealized at the expense of not only the uniformly oafish white characters but also the savage Pawnees.

Clearly what is at work here is language, which is the raw material of myth. Language is corrupted by the propagation of legends which do not jibe with the facts of history, and once corrupted it further corrupts historical understanding in rather the same way that the language of politics, as George Orwell described it in a famous essay, corrupts politics and is corrupted by it. But the fashionable nonsense which presently permeates so much discussion of texts in our universities hardly can be said to improve on that process. Of course readers of historical texts too often believe only what they want to believe. But this sorry situation hardly justifies the assumption that a historical text, like any other, is a subject fit only for its "deconstruction," substituting for what is assumed to be the word-created subjectivity of the writer the word-created subjectivity of the reader. The result of such an enterprise can only be the denial that there is such a thing as a historical fact outside the text upon which anything in the text depends.

Orwell's *1984*, if we read it with care, casts a bright light into this academic midnight. The tendency to regard it as a satire on totalitarianism misses the point that its real subject is both language and the way revolutionaries inevitably seek to impose a redefinition of language, making words mean whatever they have the power to make society think they mean. Winston Smith, after all, is not only a victim of "Newspeak" ("Peace is war," and so on) but of the constant rewriting of history to conform to what the "Ministry of Truth" happens to say it is. This is pretty much the situation at Williams College, at least recently, where one undergraduate dumbbell, undoubtedly parroting a dumbbell professor, said that the Holocaust may not have happened but was "a perfectly reasonable conceptual hallucination" (Shalit 37). In other words, the study of history at Williams College, at least in this case, brings a student finally to where, without having to pay expensive tuition, neo-Nazis begin: the Holocaust didn't happen. Here, as in *1984*, history is only what a political -- or academic -- "Big Brother" says it is, and academic "Newspeak" demands the absolute destruction of the assumption, validated both by tradition and by common sense, that historical truth is possible.

Unfortunately American Indian writers and their non-Indian allies too often have succumbed to the temptation to manipulate history to create legends of their own.

A convenient starting-point for investigating this matter is the report prepared in 1970 by Rupert Costo and Jeannette Henry on their examination of three hundred American history textbooks to determine how well they presented the full complexity of Indian roles in American history and culture. Though not one of those books met their standards, no one can quarrel with their criteria, all of which were of three kinds: factual accuracy, a fair description of the reality of present-day Indian life, and the recognition of the cultural significance of Indian peoples.

The last of these concerns is particularly significant. The truth of the matter is that we tend too often to assume that Indian America was "primitive" and that Europe was civilized and technologically advanced, and that, as a result, the long war for domination of the New World was one-sided. This is true enough for British colonies once the long conflict with France for the domination of North America was settled at Quebec in 1759, and thus it is true for the United States. But in the beginning things were more nearly even. Certainly over-simplifications about Indian impotence and European power in 1492 are shattered not only by Inca and Aztec examples but also by overwhelming evidence that Europe by the last decade of the fifteenth century was in decline, its death rate incredibly high, its population only gradually recovering from the devastation of the Black Death a century and a half before, its southeastern frontier a scene of perpetual warfare with the Ottoman Turks (who besieged Vienna as late as 1683), its primeval forests largely destroyed, and its soil over-used and increasingly unproductive. The exploration and exploitation of Europe's "new" world in the aftermath of the first voyage of Columbus made possible the development, economic but also political and intellectual, which saved Europe from a decline which before 1492 must have been inevitable.

Obviously Costo and Henry's questions point in the right direction. But in the more than two decades since they asked them we have seen the appearance of new legends which have corrupted efforts to reach an understanding of what really happened in the European conquest of America. Scholarly interest in the Indian has provided many writers, Indian and non-Indian, with the opportunity to ratify their own political and cultural assumptions. "Ethnohistorians," for example, have argued that colonial observers only noted those aspects of Indian life that confirmed their own presuppositions, and yet the conclusions of these same "ethnohistorians" often seem to suggest that they also only can see the Indian they want to see. Kirkpatrick Sale's account of the Columbian encounter, *The Conquest of Paradise* (1990), in belittling everything European, seems to be inspired by a strident environmentalism in the name of an Indian ideal of living with the land which, given the last five centuries, cannot be realized.

Other examples of the political manipulation of American Indian history are common. One is the use of *genocide* as a label for the destruction of much of the pre-Columbian population, an example of the way the corruption of language and the manipulation or even invention of historical fact go hand in hand. Indians and others writing about white-Indian relations in the past and even in the present often toss off the word automatically. Russell Means, for example, quotes an 1858 federal treaty with the Yankton Sioux which provided that annuity payments would be halted and "other [suitable and proper] provisions [would] be made" if the Yanktons did not make "reasonable and satisfactory efforts to advance and improve their condition ...." His response to the bell he hears in this language is as automatic as the saliva of

Pavlov's dog: "Advance and improve. Other provisions. Suitable and proper. Genocide" (5).

Of course, rhetorical use of *genocide* and *holocaust* was pervasive in the context of preparations for the recognition of the five hundredth anniversary of the first voyage of Columbus. We have cited (in Chapter II) Paula Gunn Allen's trivialization of the murder of six million Jews in loose talk about "a brutal holocaust that seeks to wipe us out" and "millions" of Indians slaughtered in the twenty-five years after the Civil War, but her wild charges, for which a search of documents will discover no historical moorings, are hardly unique. An influential book by Tzvetlan Todorov, *The Conquest of America* (1982), also employs numbers arbitrarily -- twenty percent of the world's population in the Americas in 1500, seven-eighths of that American total exterminated within fifty years -- to charge the first Europeans in America with genocide and to claim that "none of the great massacres of the twentieth century can be compared to this hecatomb" (133).

But in *American Holocaust* (1992) David E. Stannard's thesis not only derives from moral indignation at the slaughter of the pre-Columbian population of the Americas, understood in terms of the most radical recent estimates of its extent and the assumption that the "holocaust" killed 95% of it, but from an equivalent anger expressed in his primary premise. His villain is Christianity and its alleged attitudes toward sex, race, and war. The "American holocaust" had common origins with the Nazi Holocaust, Stannard claims, and also with American intervention in Southeast Asia and the Middle East. Christianity, allegedly, not only made Hitler slaughter Jews -- "I can't help it. I'm a Christian" -- but made Americans muck about in Vietnam and the Persian Gulf.

The trouble with this is that the population of the western hemisphere in 1492 could not possibly have been as large as the genocide peddlers would have us believe. David Henige has made the point that the "high counters" have been guilty of incredible naivete in their acceptance of the numbers found in accounts by early Spanish chroniclers and, in some cases, of incompetence (at best) in their interpretation of them. One of them, Henry F. Dobyns, for example, assumes that in the sixteenth century sixty priests in Mexico annually baptized 2,184,000 Indians. That works out to 36,400 for each priest or, ignoring leap years and working at it every day, almost a hundred a day or (and this is assuming that they never slept), one about every fifteen minutes. (Were they doing anything else?) In other words, a figure like this is strained by the same load that makes us doubt that the Aztecs really sacrificed as many victims as the priests of Cortez, who of course had every reason to exaggerate, said they did -- logistics. But where does Dobyns get this figure? It is based on his reading of several claims by the early Mexican historian Motolinia on the number of baptisms by apparently superhuman priests in the years following the conquest. One claim is that two priests baptized 14,200 Indians in five days, another way of saying that each of them, if he went 120 hours without sleep, baptized (approximately) one Indian every minute. Another figure -- one priest, no sleep, one day, fourteen thousand baptisms, i.e. one every six seconds -- is too wild even for Dobyns, but he is willing to accept another of Motolinia's assertions -- one priest, ten thousand in one day and thus one every 8.5 seconds -- and, estimating that there were sixty priests in Mexico at that time, he concludes that there had to be more than two million baptisms a year and thus an enormous Mexican population after the Conquest and presumably even more before it (Henige 175).

Perhaps the only crime here is gullibility -- or the lack of a pocket calculator -- but Henige cites a couple of other "high counters," Woodrow Borah and Sherburne Cook, in a case which suggests something less forgivable. They have concluded that the pre-Columbian population of Hispaniola must have been at least three million. Why? They cite the early account of Las Casas, who says in one place that the island's population was "many" millions and in six others that it was three million. That's good enough for Borah and Cook, who neglect to mention *even once* that Las Casas also says *in five other places* that Hispaniola's original population was *one* million (182-183). Obviously Las Casas didn't really know how many Indians were in Hispaniola in 1492, and obviously Borah and Cook believe what they want to believe.

Since such selective reading of historical documents cannot derive from a disinterested pursuit of truth we must suspect that it is a product of the political culture of its time. As John Daniels has pointed out, the remarkable increase in estimates of the pre-Columbian population of the Americas -- and thus the extent of the slaughter of most of it even before permanent settlements had been achieved in what is now the United States -- accompanied the rise in the Vietnam "body count": "we" were slaughtering non-white people in Vietnam just as "we" slaughtered them in the sixteenth century.

Or consider, as another example, *The Missions of California: A Legacy of Genocide* (1987), another book edited by Costo and Henry, which appeared in the context of the Vatican's consideration of Father Juniperro Serra for sainthood. The editors and their writers argue that Serra should not be canonized because his disruption of Indian culture and society in the creation of the California missions was genocidal. They actually compare the mission system with Nazi Germany and the alleged culpability of Serra with that of the Nazi defendants in the Nuremberg trials.

But *genocide* is a word with an interesting history. It appeared first in 1944 in a book by one Raphael Lemkin about the Axis rule of occupied Europe. Lemkin coined the word (from Latin roots meaning *race killing*) to denote the planned and coordinated destruction of entire national, religious, or racial groups. Obviously he was referring primarily to the Nazi slaughter of European Jews, and the denotation he gave to his word, and its clear etymology, was implied in the official condemnation in 1946 by the General Assembly of the United Nations of "the denial of the right to existence to entire human groups." Then in 1948 the UN's Genocide Convention was adopted with language which indicated that *genocide* could be defined not only as the planned destruction of life on a mass scale but also as causing "mental harm" to members of a group. This trend continued until in 1990 a book on *The History and Sociology of Genocide* (by Frank Chalk and Kurt Jonassohn) could say that genocide was not only a matter of physical destruction but of *any* attack on the liberty, dignity, personal security, culture, language, and national feelings of the members of a group (Stannard 279-280). From this it is only a simple step to our present muddle. If you don't like the way your group is being treated you can get away with saying that that treatment is genocidal. In other words, yet another good word is dissolving in the political muck.

But we really ought to find other ways to label cultural oppression so as to retain the original usefulness of the word *genocide*, that is, the mass killing of the people of a group by a perpetrator who *intends* to destroy the group. This meaning does not cover those killed in a two-sided war, even if the sides are unequal, or a natural or unintended disaster such as an epidemic of disease, or by individuals acting *outside* the orders of any political authority or state. When the Spanish regime in the West Indies is condemned both for enslaving Indians and for waging genocide by means of disease, we ought to remember that though Spanish slave-masters certainly committed atrocities against some of their slaves in order to command the obedience of the rest of them it was obviously in the slave-master's interest to keep his slaves alive if he could, that that interest eliminates any *deliberate* intention to wipe them out as a people, that a true genocidal campaign must be *planned*, and that in any case the smallpox and other diseases which caused the greatest loss of life were also a problem for the Spanish and almost as great a mystery for them as they were for the Indians. James Axtell makes the point that except for a few episodes -- he cites the campaign against the Pequods in 1637 and that of the French against the Fox tribe in the 1730's -- there are few examples of true genocide in the history of the conquest of North America (*Beyond* 1492, 261). (He might also have mentioned the successful campaign by white settlers in northern California in the 1860's to exterminate the Yana tribe -- or for that matter that of the Iroquois against the Hurons in 1649.) When we muddle the terminology, therefore, we trivialize the Jewish Holocaust and very likely cause many readers who might otherwise be outraged over the plight of the Mission Indians, for example, to drop the subject.

But it is not likely that anything can be done to save *genocide* and *holocaust*, which are obviously useful terms, from those who use them to describe anything they dislike in the way their group is being treated. The problem remains with the substitution of legend for history, and the Spanish "black legend" is evolving into a larger European (and white American) black legend.

Needless to say, this process includes a convenient ignoring of certain pre-Columbian realities. Consider, for example, the Spanish conquest of Mexico. The fashionable version of this incredible story is that believed by the people and even the government of Mexico, the story which has been enshrined in the murals of Diego Rivera. Supposedly the Spanish were able to enslave the Indians of Mexico because they had the advantage of gunpowder and artillery and because they were assisted by Malinche, the "traitor" who betrayed her own people by serving Cortez as translator. When we consider this woman as an actual historical figure we well may wonder where the feminists are when we really need them. After all, Malinche knew the language of the Mayans as well as her own Nahuatl, the language of the Aztecs, only because Aztecs had sold her into slavery. She owed the Aztecs absolutely nothing, and she threw in with Cortez for legitimate personal reasons: he freed her from slavery. As for the conquest itself, Cortez had many things going for him, including the incredible coincidence that he came to Mexico in 1519, which happened to be One Reed, the year which the Aztecs believed might see the return of the god Quetzalcoatl and an overthrow of the official religion of human sacrifice -- which, ironically, is what Cortez, in his role as Quetzalcoatl, actually did. But Cortez had very little artillery, and few of his men had firearms. They had steel armor but it was uncomfortable to wear in the Mexican heat and they soon abandoned it for the quilted armor of their enemies. And except for a few arquebusiers, crossbowmen, and mounted lancers most of them fought on foot with edged weapons against Mexican warriors who fought on foot with edged weapons. But except for smallpox, introduced into Mexico accidentally and without any intent that can be documented, the only real Spanish advantage was in the anger of the people of Tlaxcala, who for decades had been at war with the Mexica of Tenochtitlan and who, after an initial resistance, allied with the Spanish and contributed thousands of warriors to the war against the Mexica. It can be argued that the Tlaxcalans finally were able to realize their long dream of overthrowing the Aztec empire only when the Spanish tipped the balance of power in central Mexico.

But the tendency toward the creation of new legends in our revisionist era not only produces claims for European and white American villainy. Anyone who thinks that every evil done in the last five centuries must be European and white will also find it easy to assume that anything of value that has been accomplished in those five centuries must be less European and white than conventional history has suggested. An example is the frequently repeated claim, considered proven by most Indians, that the United States Constitution was directly influenced by the structure of the Iroquois League. Molly Brant, in an imagined address to the Founding Fathers in Maurice Kenny's poetic reconstruction of her life, claims just that:

> If I could scratch figures
> I would show you the fathers of Thirteen Fires ...
> how you took up the wisdom
> of our great and wise Peacemaker ....
> If you would listen ...
> you would remember always
> where your freedoms and liberties
> first captured your attention (130).

We must not quarrel too much with this; it is after all the speech of a character in a poem, not the thought of the historical Molly Brant, which cannot be known, but of the Molly Brant who is the product of Kenny's imagination and is thus not subject to the rules of historical evidence. Still the historical inaccuracy which prompts it must be noted.

Presumably the thrust of Kenny's argument is that the "freedoms and liberties" to which his Molly Brant refers -- meaning, presumably, those guaranteed by the Bill of Rights -- originated in the Iroquois system of government which allegedly inspired the federal system defined in the Constitution which made the Bill of Rights possible. In fact, the structure of matriarchal clans and League council and that council's parliamentary procedures bear no resemblance whatever to the structure of the Constitution. In a characteristic diatribe the Mohawk poet Peter Blue Cloud admitted as much even as he made the conventional claim.

> Talk about ... this so-called [*sic*] United States government. A lot of it is based on the Six Nations, but they left out all the important parts like the Clan Mothers, like the Council of Elders, like the Chiefs .... If they'd really chosen wise men to run the country and women to be behind them like the Clan Mothers, ... maybe it would have worked (Bruchac, *Survival* 37).

The truth, of course, is that if the Clan Mothers, Council, and Chiefs are left out, there is no "lot of it" in the United States Constitution that was "based on the Six Nations."

Thanks to activists who mounted a major campaign in 1987 to make a "statement" in the context of the Bicentennial of the Constitution, the United States Congress (in U.S. Senate Concurrent Resolution 76, Sept. 16, 1987) endorsed this particular Indian legend, passing a resolution which declares that both the Articles of Confederation and the Constitution actually were modelled on the principles of the Iroquois League (Clifton, "Alternate Identities" 2). Apparently it's too much to ask politicians to care for the truth when a few votes might be at stake, but the fact happens to be that, as Elisabeth Tooker has pointed out, a search of seventeenth and eighteenth century documents reveals very little exact description of just how the Iroquois League was governed. Indeed nothing of any particular value about the actual mechanics of its government found its way into print until 1847, when the first articles on the subject were published by Lewis Henry Morgan (311).

What is clear in the history of the League and the history of the creation of the Constitution is that at various times in the thirty years before the Constitution was drafted various political figures, on at least one occasion an Iroquois chief, argued in the context of Britain's war with France for control of North America that some sort of union of Britain's American colonies was desirable. The idea of union, well before it was stated as a desirable goal in the Preamble of the Constitution, was extolled by various colonial leaders who said, as did Benjamin Franklin, that it would be unfortunate if a union were not achieved, considering the fact that "these savages" (the Iroquois) had been able to achieve theirs.

But the idea of union is not uniquely Iroquois. And even if political union had never been heard of in the world until the Iroquois thought of it, claims for Iroquois influence on the Constitution still would have to be supported by evidence that the structure of the federal government and the Constitutional definitions of political power upon which that government is based were somehow derived from Iroquois example.

Scholars who have argued for Iroquois influence on the Founding Fathers have cited a variety of eighteenth-century American political thinkers whose references to Indian government often seem more rhetorical than substantive, and they place considerable weight upon coincidence. Donald Grinde, in a recent summary of the arguments, cites a statement by John Adams to the effect that "every nation in North America has a king, a senate, and a people" (a dubious claim in itself), to justify his own assertion that the structure of "king," sachems, and council is evidence of a "wisdom of balance and separation of powers in American Indian governments." For Grinde, the Constitution derives from "American Indian notions of confederation, federalism, separation of powers, and the unification of vast geographic expanses under a noncolonial government ..." (164, 166). But one Indian scholar who believes the Iroquois legend, Vine Deloria, Jr., has sneered at Tooker's argument that, in his words, "no one, not even the Indians, knew anything about the Six Nations form of government until the anthropologists wrote it down" (403). A reading of Tooker's article will make it clear that she says nothing of the kind, and a reading of Deloria's statement will make equally clear that he quite dishonestly has used her reasonable argument that nothing was available in print to give the Founding Fathers any idea of how the Iroquois League governed itself to take a conventionally snotty swipe at anthropolgists. Of course, the Iroquois knew how the

League operated. But if no Iroquois went to Philadelphia in 1787 to advise the Founding Fathers and if no Founding Father ever sat in on a meeting of the Iroquois Council and if no non-Iroquois could know how the thing worked until Morgan published what Iroquois informants told him about it, where is the Iroquois influence on the Constitution? Deloria criticizes what he calls Tooker's "appalling" ignorance of political philosophy, the evidence for which, he says, is her assumption that Locke, rather than Montesquieu, was the greatest influence on the Constitution. If only, he says, she had bothered to read *The Federalist*.... Of course, he's right about Montesquieu, and Grinde's "American Indian notions" are actually those addressed in those writings of Montesquieu which most influenced the Constitutional convention. But Deloria may not be as smart as he thinks he is for bringing up *The Federalist*. If the Founding Fathers got *any* of their stuff from the Iroquois you would think that somewhere in that bible of Constitutional thought we would be able to find some mention of the Iroquois League. Various confederacies and political unions are mentioned in *The Federalist* -- most of them from the history of ancient Greece -- and the British government and constitution provide references, by my count, in thirty-four of the eighty-five essays. But how many references can we find to the Iroquois League? Not one.

And in any case, Deloria has missed the crucial point in the implications of what he is saying: if Montesquieu, not Locke, was the primary influence on the Constitution, then the Iroquois were not.

On the other hand, though Bruce Johansen's argument seems rather limp when he suggests that the relation of the "younger" Iroquois nations (Cayuga, Oneida) to the "older" (Mohawk, Seneca) "somewhat resembled that of a two-house congress in one body ..." and that "the Onandagas filled something of an executive role ..." (25), his claims for generally Indian influences on the development of American notions of political freedom proceed from a premise which is worth considering. It is that the creation of the colonial society out of which the United States emerged was from the beginning the result of the inter-penetration of

European and Indian elements and that this process continued as Indian and white American (and he might have added African American) elements merged to produce the larger American culture which we know.

Unquestionably the ideal of individual freedom was, at least in part, an Indian contribution to the development of European political thought. As William Brandon has made clear, American Indian examples, or more precisely the idealization of those examples in what European observers of America wrote for European audiences, made possible the development of that ideal: "the Old World was subtly infected by reports from the New to the point that tangled New World influences appear to be dominant in certain of our own social ideas today" (3). It is reasonable to assume, in other words, that the European perception of America as a place without Europe's past, a place, that is, without sin, a place where the savages were noble and the landscape Edenic and thus a place where Europeans could start over and perhaps return to the simplicity of a Golden Age inspired Jefferson's frequent references to all that was wrong with "old Europe" as well as his notion of "the laws of nature and of nature's god."

Furthermore, this commerce in ideas and ideals accompanied the commercial exploitation of America's natural resources. The idea of freedom was a reaction to the growth of absolute monarchy, and that growth resulted from the destruction of feudalism and from the undermining of the restraints of the Church. When the state became so rich from American gold and silver that the Church could no longer oppose it, the state could afford to become oppressive. With the oppression came new ideas of individual freedom derived from examples discovered in America's landscape and people.

In any case, when we study the early history of Europe's encounter with America we would do well to understand what really happened in the beginning of this country's history. Small groups of Europeans landed on American shores and encountered small and sometimes rather large groups of Indians. The peacefulness of these first encounters were, in fact, as often as not due to the fact that these first settlers were vastly out-numbered by those they encountered. But subsequent increases in the population of the invaders made war inevitable. And the first wars were not always one-sided. That fought by the Virginians against the Powhatan Confederacy was, if anything, one-sided in the other direction, and in 1622 the Indians very nearly wiped out the colony. The Europeans in any case understood what they were doing in the light of their recent experience at home -- the centuries-long Spanish *reconquista* of Moorish territory and the English wars against the wild Scots and Irish and their colonization of their conquered territories. William MacLeod's argument in regard to the latter phenomenon is long-established. In 1600 the Celtic peoples of Ireland and the Scottish Highlands were politically on the level of the Indians of North America and well below that of the Aztecs and Incas. Their population density was less than that of almost the entire North American continent and perhaps as small as one-eighth that of England and the rest of Scotland. Except for their cattle herds they were as primitive in agriculture as most agricultural Indian tribes. The English response to these people resembles unfortunate aspects of the conflict of whites and Indians in North America, including calls for extermination, the Plantation of Ulster in 1609 (an almost exact equivalent of the "plantation" of Virginia), and systems not unlike the later American reservation system (152-171).

As the continent was subdued, economic realities affected the way Indian tribes formed alliances with each other or with the invaders. When, for example, the Iroquois found that they had become dependent on European trade goods (particularly guns, powder, and shot) and that they had trapped out their own territory, they inevitably became an imperialist power, pursuing bloody wars, often wars of extermination, with the Hurons, the Eries, the Illini, and other tribes. Another example is the remarkable success of the Sioux in dominating the territory -- and the trade -- of the northern Great Plains in the late eighteenth and early nineteenth century. As Robert White has shown, the wars fought by the Sioux against their neighbors were motivated not by emotions felt for their ancestral homeland -- they were interlopers on the plains -- but by an understandable desire to monopolize buffalo herds, which provided not only their primary food but the basis for their commercial relations with white traders. And the wars were bloody. In 1804 Sioux warriors killed half of the people in a Ponca village in a single raid and seventy-five Omahas in another, and a Sioux party killed a hundred Pawnees in an 1873 battle (326, 339). By modern standards these numbers may seem paltry, but they certainly go beyond our usual assumption that plains warriors really were motivated only by the desire to acquire battlefield honors by "counting coup."

In other words, the English and the French were for a hundred years at war with a number of small powers in North America, allied with others, and at war with each other, and they, and the Iroquois and Sioux, achieved empire for the reason that "civilized" nations usually go to war -- for profound geopolitical interests, or, if one prefers, for loot and conquest. The truth is that the records of all nations reveal similar responses to historical circumstances. What the Iroquois and Sioux did to their neighbors, what the English and French did to theirs and to each other in North America, and what Americans did in the West in the nineteenth century is what the Anglo-Saxons did to the Britons in the latter half of the fifth century and what the Normans did to the Anglo-Saxons after 1066.

What is required, in other words, is mutual understanding, a measure of humility, and a recognition of a common humanity in the records of nations which reveal origins and developments which are more alike than we may wish to believe.

Such a recognition will prevent a great deal of sentimentality when we hear the historical Indian put forth as environmental saint. Father DeSmet, who was on the Great Plains in 1848, estimated that in that one year the Sioux shipped 25,000 buffalo tongues and 110,000 robes down the Missouri to St. Louis (White 330). Almost no whites were in the Dakotas at that time, so this slaughter of buffalo derived not from the corruption of the morals of the Sioux by white neighbors but from their willingness to exploit their primary natural resource -- accompanied by a willingness to go to war with other tribes to protect their range. But the Sioux were not the first to exploit their natural resources wastefully for economic advantage. In the sixteenth century the Mahicans in a single year sold 46,000 beaver pelts to the Dutch, and the Hurons in the middle of that century were producing thirty thousand annually. In the mid-eighteenth century Charleston, South Carolina was exporting an average of 152,000 deerskins annually, the Cherokees killing 1.25 million deer for this trade between 1739 and 1759 (Axtell, *Beyond* 1492, 130-131). The economic reasons for this slaughter are much easier to perceive than any particular moral superiority that can be defined in the light of ecological concern.

If we want to blame bad white influences for it we might ask just what happened to Cahokia? That great concentration of people in the neighborhood of present-day East St. Louis was a major city, a commercial center, and the site of remarkable mound temples. It collapsed in the early sixteenth century, long before any European had a chance to see it. Why? Was it conquered by some less civilized tribe? Or, as seems more likely, were the surrounding agricultural fields worn out by over-planting? To put it another way, is it not likely that the fall of Cahokia, like that of various cities of the Middle East -- or of the Hohokam culture of southern Arizona -- was due to its inhabitants' inadequate grasp of principles of agronomy not discovered by Europeans or anyone else until several centuries later?

Much of the legend-making of recent years, when it is reduced to its primary elements, reveals evidence of the continued presence in our culture of the "noble savage." The assumption that Indians did not know how to scalp their enemies until Europeans taught them how to do it, for another example, implies that Indians were noble savages too innocent to have figured out anything like scalping without being led astray by evil Europeans. The truth of the matter is that James Axtell has cited enough arguments to demonstrate that Indians did not have to be taught by Europeans how to scalp ("Unkindest Cut"). For example, the languages of tribes on the Atlantic seaboard contained many words, none of them loan words from European languages, for *scalp*, *to scalp*, and *scalping*. For another, it is a fact that though European soldiers were notorious for desecrating enemy dead in the European wars of the sixteenth and seventeenth centuries, it also is a fact that no historical record indicates that they scalped them. Archaeological and historical records provide further evidence that Indian claims that "we didn't scalp until you taught us how to do it" are based less on fact than on desire.

In any case, we ought to remember that the idea that civilization corrupts and that savagery is too innocent a state to be really savage is much older than Rousseau. In another version it informs the description of the ancient Germans in the writings of Tacitus. Those Germans were hardly more advanced socially, culturally, and politically than most Indian tribes in 1492 (and were less advanced than some), and we will come nearer to the truth if we remember that the origins of *all* nations are in "savagery." Were the Germans of Tacitus too "noble" and innocent to scalp? If so, when did their descendants take up scalping so that it could be passed on to Indians later? And who taught those descendants? And in any case why did Indians take to it so easily?

Or consider the matter of Iroquois torture of prisoners. Costo and Henry more or less imply that it may never have occurred: "Examining the original sources, we find ... that they are usually dependent on the Jesuit relations" (*Textbooks* 169). And in another context they say that the Jesuit reports were "phonied up for adaptation to the original Catholic concept of the Indian as a subhuman being ..." (*Textbooks* 154). But this hardly reflects Jesuit assumptions. Indeed one historian, George R. Healy, has found a clear line of influence from the Jesuit reports to the writings of the eighteenth century French philosophers who developed the concept of the "noble savage." And in any case the Roman Catholic church settled the question in favor of Indian humanity relatively early in the Spanish experience in the West Indies, long before French Jesuits first visited the Iroquois. And it should be mentioned in this context that the first English settlers did not assume that Indians were even of a different race, let alone a different species. As Alden Vaughan has made clear in an exhaustive article, those colonists through much of the seventeenth century -- until the French wars, largely because of the brutality of Indian auxiliaries, had become incredibly bloody -- assumed almost universally that Indians were descended from the Ten Lost Tribes of Israel and were thus practically Europeans, and that their dark complexions, which apparently were not even noticed by many first observers, were a natural result of spending so much time outdoors ("From White Man to Redskin").

If we want a true account of the phenomenon of torture, we ought not to waste time impugning Jesuit motives. Those Jesuits who witnessed burnings at the stake were appalled less by the horror of it -- their doctrine, after all, had prepared them to confront human depravity -- than by what they considered the trivial (that is, political, military, or merely social, rather than religious) motives of the executioners. After all, when the Iroquois burned prisoners at the stake they were only doing what was being done at the same time to religious heretics and "witches" in many parts of Europe.

To date, no one has tried to claim that the Iroquois and other Eastern tribes burned captives at the stake only after Europeans taught them how to do it. But rather than inventing another legend to this effect we would do well to realize that the past of no nation will bear much examination by those who wish to believe that they are descended from saints.

In any case, for what further development of American myth may we hope? Is it possible that the American people might possess the collective wisdom to discover in their history and culture a yet untold myth which might unify the disparate elements of our society and help to create a unified and healthier American consciousness? To put it another way, may we hope that an American nationality is possible? And if it is not, can we really be certain that American society will survive?

CHAPTER VII

AMERICAN MYTH, YET UNTOLD

In the quinticentennial observance of the first voyage of Columbus much appropriately was made of the contribution of America to Europe in the aftermath of that event, and charges of genocide were made by Indians -- and also by those Americans who sought to ease their burden of guilt for sins committed by others. Indian America, according to the rhetoric, gave Europe maize, potatoes, and chocolate, to say nothing of enormous wealth in Peruvian gold and Mexican silver, and received in return a terrible panoply of bacteria which, according to the fashionable estimate, wiped out ninety-five per cent of the enormous population of an Eden which until then had been free of disease.

In the previous chapter I suggested my own assumptions about modern estimations of the extent of the pre-Columbian population, so I will say nothing about it here. And in any case I see no point in the sort of contests well-meaning, idealistic people get into when they feel the need to prove their sensitivity to the imperfections revealed in the history of Indian-white relations.

What we need is a more thorough examination of the nature of the exchange of goods, particularly the intellectual and spiritual goods, produced by the European encounter with America. An argument easily can be made that the impact of America on Europe took form in the rise of modern capitalism, fueled originally by the wealth of American mines; in the Reformation, which shook the foundations of church authority by posing questions which Scripture could not answer; and in the concept of individualism, which derived from new conceptions of human liberty. The discovery in America of new realities -- new natural phenomena but, more important, new societies and peoples -- produced great philosophical changes in Europe because those new realities required reappraisals of what constituted civilization and human nature. The European response to this new world inevitably was couched in terms that were by 1492 venerable in European mythology and tradition -- the Golden Age, the Garden of Eden, and the universalist assumptions of Greek and Roman philosophy and of Christianity itself. In other words, the foundations of what later became the ideals of rationalism, of progress, of individual freedom, and indeed of every other philosophical justification of self-government were present in European thought in 1492, but modern political thought could not be built upon them until the philosophical foundations of Europe had been shaken by its cataclysmic encounter with America.

To put it another way, if the transformation of America by Europe was total and radical, so was the transformation of Europe by America. Indeed the history of the world since 1492 is a history of the inter-penetration of Europe and America, with everything else -- even the rise of India, China, and Japan and the colonization of Africa -- an addendum to the history of the integration of the "new world" and the "old." This perception of the influence not only of Europe on Indian America but of Indian America on Europe is at the heart of the argument of the Canadian sociologist Jean-Jacques Simard that, in fact, the terms *Indian* and *White* are virtually meaningless for understanding what the people concerned really are. Ever since the seventeenth and eighteenth centuries, he argues, the terms have been "entangled in the collective thought of both European and New World peoples.... For this reason, to understand what it means to be an Indian in the contemporary world would require, also, knowing what it means to be a Whiteman." Therefore, Simard argues, with a phrase useful for defining the vital relationship of writing by Indian authors to American literature as a whole, the culture of Native American peoples is "the Whiteman's shadow" (333).

Obviously this notion that Indians and whites can only understand themselves in their relation to each other is at odds with contemporary claims of ethnic uniqueness and with the assumption that perpetual confrontation is the most appropriate stance for minority cultures. Simard suggests not only that "the Whiteman" can only know himself if he realizes that he is to a degree an Indian but also that "the Indian" can only know himself if he realizes that he is to a degree white. And though this development of a "mixed" consciousness has from the beginning been accompanied by much racial "mixing," Simard is not really talking about "blood." The fact is that for the past five hundred years America has been the scene of a complex process of cultural inter-penetration which still continues and which must be understood if we are to know what we mean by an American consciousness.

Considering the great stake that Indian writers have in defining the ways their work is different from the mainstream of American literature, it is remarkable that so many of them acknowledge their obligations and allegiance to that mainstream. The great majority of them, whatever they have learned about a tribal culture from their own experience, have also discovered that culture by reading the work of non-Indian scholars. For example, as we have seen, Momaday's work is not only informed by his thorough education in British and American literary traditions, but the origins of *The Way to Rainy Mountain* are not only in Kiowa story-telling but in Momaday's reading of James Mooney's *Calendar History of the Kiowa Indians*.

Of course, the complaints of Indians about the way they have been treated by anthropologists are often, if not usually, legitimate, though much of what they detest in that treatment is inevitable, given the scientific ideal of objectivity. Unfortunately the complaint of Indians against anthropologists has affected their attitudes toward scholarship in general, and even more unfortunately these more general attitudes have had their effect, baleful in my opinion, on the development of Indian attitudes toward fiction and poetry written by Indians themselves. Daniel Littlefield, surveying these processes in the light of his experience as a co-editor of a classroom anthology of American literature, has noted that Indian writers themselves are in disagreement over the basic question of whether writing by Indians should be part of the American "canon." As he says, some of them (Momaday, Louise Erdrich) consider this writing a part of American literature as a whole. But others "believe that their literature is distinct in the use of language and the themes it portrays" and that those Littlefield calls "we" cannot understand their writing because we are ignorant of American Indian cultures (104-105). He cites as an example of this argument a statement by Robert Allen Warrior that because Indian writing is, or ought to be, "anti-colonial" it can be explored less meaningfully as an element in "the national literature of the United States" than in comparison to African, African-American, or Arab "literatures of resistance" (105).

But this perception of the duties of scholarship has spilled over into some Indian attitudes toward the poetry and fiction Indians write. Elizabeth Cook-Lynn has chosen to divide Indian writers according to whether they "[look] out on the white world from a communal, tribally specific indigenous past" (75) or, presumably, examine tribal societies the way non-Indians only can examine them -- from the outside. But this distinction can by no means be applied simply to the body of Indian writing, and Cook-Lynn's attempt to do so clearly is based on a racial definition. Those she calls "urban mixed-blood" Indians -- she cites some of the most significant writers in the Indian "Renaissance," among them Maurice Kenny, Thomas King, Wendy Rose, and Gerald Vizenor -- are, she says, "the major self-described mixed-blood voices of the decade," tellers of "the so-called 'mixed-blood' story, often called 'the post-colonial' story [of the] bicultural nature of Indian lives ..." (67). As far as she is concerned, this "mixed-blood" literature is characterized by "excesses of individualism" which are at odds with "the tribal communal story [and] an ongoing tribal literary tradition," by a lack of faith in "a return to tribal sovereignty on Indian homelands" (69), and, in fact, by complicity in the marginalization of "the structural political problems facing the First Nations in America ..." (71).

It's hard to know what to make of such an argument, given the fact that the work of those "writers who do not situate themselves within the mixed-blood or mainstream spectrum" -- she cites among others Vine Deloria, Jr., N. Scott Momaday, Leslie Marmon Silko, and Ray Young Bear (75) -- originates in the same combination of tribal experience and historical and ethnological study that we find in those writers she condemns. Indeed, this combination is so typical of so many Indian writers that it is not easy to know what to make of Peter Blue Cloud's dismissal of Lewis Henry Morgan and other ethnologists who have studied the Iroquois. When he was asked in an interview whether these writers had added to our knowledge of the Iroquois, Blue Cloud said they had not. But his muddled understanding of what he was talking about is clear in his claim that anyone who *really* wanted to know about the Iroquois people should read Edmund Wilson, "who was so impressed with what he found that he went out and talked to live people" (Bruchac, *Survival* 36). The truth is that such a statement suggests that Blue Cloud, if he ever has read Morgan, paid little attention to what he was reading because Morgan obviously had to interview "live people" to find out what he wrote about the Iroquois League. And for that matter Blue Cloud also does not seem to have read Wilson's *Apologies to the Iroquois* (1960), considering the fact that Wilson clearly based his book not only on what "live people" told him but on what he read in the sources which he honestly acknowledged -- Speck, Fenton, Hewitt, Anthony Wallace, Arthur Parker, and, as a matter of fact, Lewis Henry Morgan.

I am convinced that, for all the legitimacy of Indian demands that all writers treat tribal cultures honestly we will never really understand writing by Indian authors if we assume that it is *only* tribal. The fact of the matter is that that writing and the total American culture which it illuminates and from which, to one degree or another, it derives are so entangled with each other that they cannot be separated. As Momaday has said, the Indian has been a constant presence in American literature from the beginning, and, as we have seen, American culture as a whole has profoundly affected even that literary expression that is considered the most characteristically Indian.

In the present muddle of incomplete myth and false legend -- to say nothing of incredible public ignorance of history -- what is needed is a great exercise in syncretism if not by our people as a whole, then at least by our intellectuals, who allegedly are smarter, if not wiser, than the public at large. In the previous chapter I referred to the American myth of democracy and individual freedom which has been operative for two centuries. Clearly what is wrong with that myth is that it is too Euro-American, which is to say that it is narrowly progressive, it is oriented only toward the future, it ignores the claims of the past and thus denies tragedy, and it reveals no interest whatever in the fate of those who were defeated to make possible what believers in the myth consider progress. We would do well to remember Walt Whitman's willingness -- in "Song of Myself" -- to chant a song not only for the victors but for the vanquished. We have been able to make a place in our pantheon of heroes for Robert E. Lee because we have recognized his nobility in defeat. We must do the same for our Indian heroes. As Alexander Adams says in his biography of Geronimo, the spirit of the Apaches "lives wherever men and women are struggling against overwhelming odds for freedom and justice. We, as Americans, should be proud that the Apaches' story is part of our country's heritage" (23).

It is in this light that we ought to consider the so-called canon war which has been waged for some time now in the literature departments of colleges and universities. For all of the claims of the multiculturalists that their ballyhoo about the uniqueness of female or black or Indian or Hispanic experience is on behalf of the fulfillment of the democratic promise of America, the assumption that the most significant thing about anyone is racial, ethnic or sexual actually denies individuality and thus the individualism which justifies the democratic faith. Race, ethnicity and gender remain as always mere accidents, and the determination to focus on these accidents and the assumption that racially, ethnically, and sexually identified cultures are unique and thus mutually exclusive inevitably replaces any assumption that we possess a common humanity with a belief in group "identities" which can be defined only in terms of power -- that is, politically. Indeed we can put much of this in a proper light if we realize that these professors want what Robespierres have always wanted -- to tell others what, to prove their purity, they must think and do. Furthermore, the whole enterprise ignores the sad fact, which they would not be able to ignore if they knew how to judge literary works by literary rather than by political standards, that much that is involved in human endeavor remains tragic. As Stanley Crouch has said,

> [the central idea of democracy] is that greatness can come from anywhere, that virtue knows no innate limitations, that genius and courage arrive where they will, that every group or class is as vulnerable to the shortcomings of the human species as any other. The ethnic or sexual separatist -- like the racist -- [wants] to hide from the grandeur and pressure of democracy and avoid the tragic knowledge of human frailty (68-69).

Leaving aside the fact that *canon*, with its ecclesiastical implications, is hardly the right word and that what is really being contested is the content -- and in fact the political content -- of syllabi, the thrust of those who demand a greater recognition of the diversity of American culture is appropriate. But if the call for that recognition is to mean anything more than an appeal to utter anarchy, it must mean the reconciliation of the diverse elements of our culture into a fuller, less exclusive, and more complete synthesis. University intellectuals tend to understand everything in terms of confrontation for the same reason that newspapers prefer to print bad news. Good news doesn't sell papers, and professors in our modern academy of Laputa seem to have discovered that the road to tenure, promotion, big salaries and small labor is easier for those who work to divide diverse groups than it is for those who work to unite them. But with no attempt to discover what our diverse people have in common, the result of wedging Indian, African American, female, and other elements into the syllabus to counteract and presumably replace many of the white and male elements which have dominated it will be what Harold Bloom has called "the Balkanization of literature," and the attempt to discover what American literature has been will lead to the discovery that it hasn't been very much of anything. The idea that because we are a diverse people the survey course in American literature ought also to be diverse needs to be answered by the idea that precisely *because* we are male and female, black and white and Indian, Hispanic and Asian, "straight" and otherwise, we ought to try to discover the significance of the fact that all of us also are American. As Americans what we have in common is not a "Euro-American" (and presumably white and male) "consensus" but an American consciousness that is the result of the meeting on this continent of European, Indian, and African elements. Every American, knowing it or not, is a European *and* an Indian *and* an African living in an American landscape . To be an American, in other words, is not the same thing as being a European, nor is it for that matter the same thing, even for Indians, as being an Indian in 1492. Indeed it can be argued that if no American of European descent would be alive today if Europe had never "discovered" America it is just as true that none of those who are labeled Indian in America today would be alive under those conditions. This is only one aspect of the past which we must accept. If today the two worlds of 1492 were unknown to each other, the Indians of 1492 would have descendants in the Western hemisphere and the Europeans of 1492 would have descendants in Europe, but they would not be those descendants that they actually have today. All of us -- those who call ourselves Indian in America today and those who do not -- are the result of the European encounter with America.

This is the thesis of Edward Countryman's survey of American history in the light of what he calls "the collision of histories." As he says,

> all three groups, red, white, and black, became inextricably intertwined .... [The] Natives and the Africans changed the Europeans, even as the Europeans were changing them. All became 'Americans,' and they did it because of their entanglement with all the others (4-5).

And D.H. Lawrence indicated such a vision a long time ago in *Studies in Classic American Literature* (1923), which, though in many ways a preposterous book, includes a first chapter, "The Spirit of Place," which is still worth reading. We need not go so far as to repudiate the democratic ideal, which Lawrence held in such contempt, to understand his half-optimistic belief that in spite of everything, somewhere in the American psyche was "the first hint and revelations of ... the American whole soul" (12). Our achievement of a synthesis of the discordant elements of our consciousness -- our discovery of our "whole soul" -- depends on our recognition of the interrelationship of the Indian and European and African elements that have created America and the American consciousness. It depends on substantial re-thinking of what the American myth has been and what it should become.

Certainly we will never get anywhere in an attempt to achieve an understanding of that "whole soul" by proceeding according to current definitions of "multi-ethnicity." Obviously we ought to embrace any effort to recognize contributions of individual Indians, African Americans, and others to our history and culture. But as we have said, the recent fragmentation of the "canon" of American literature gives too often a sense that there *is* no American literature, that what instead must be studied are several mutually exclusive literatures, and that the American past is not a history of a people but of several peoples in confrontations that not only have not been resolved but cannot and should not be. Surely before such a view is institutionalized in course syllabi it ought to be examined with some degree of skepticism.

Anyone who thinks my dismay excessive should take account of the work of the New York State Social Studies Syllabus Review Committee, which recommended a wholesale revision of the way social studies should be taught in New York schools, the insertion into syllabi of elements of ethnic history and culture -- with *ethnic* understood to mean *racial* -- and the deletion of "European" elements. The report of this committee was considered an improvement on that of an earlier committee which produced so much public dismay that the State School

Commissioner was forced to appoint a second committee. The first committee's report included among other absurdities the by now famous buffoonery of Professor Leonard Jeffries, Jr. about "ice people" -- whites, in other words -- who he says are violent because their skin lacks melanin. (How do we reply to the babbling of "Skinheads" about non-whites being "mud people"? With Leonard Jeffries.) The second committee, however, included, perhaps even more outrageously, Professor Ali Mazrui, a Kenyan imported by a New York state university to head an African Studies department under the terms of a contract that included all the benefits of a prestigious professorship -- tenure, a six-figure salary, and assistants to do his research for him. These benefits, however, did not excite in him any gratitude to the educational institutions which are among the products of Western civilization, which, he said in his share of the second report, is in a decline which, in the interest of "humanity" (his word) should make all of us happy.

The historian Arthur Schlesinger, a member of the second committee, dissented from what he was convinced was the wrong-headed thesis of its majority. He understood that social science syllabi ought to take account of the ethnic conflicts which keep us apart, but he argued that they also ought to take account of those forces which have held us together. The truth is that to the extent that we have maintained any political or cultural unity in America we have done so not by preserving *old* European, Indian and African identities but by working to achieve a *new* American one. Schlesinger quoted John Quincy Adams, who told a European early in the nineteenth century that "[Americans] must look forward to their posterity rather than backward to their ancestors" (630). Schlesinger's final word on the subject ought to chill the heart of anyone who really cares whether American society survives.

> I recognize that I am very much in the minority in these comments. But ... I cannot conscientiously go along with my colleagues. I ... beg them to consider what kind of nation we will have if we press further down the road to cultural separatism and ethnic fragmentation, if we institutionalize the classification of our citizens by ethnic and racial

criteria, and if we abandon our historic commitment to an American identity. What will hold our people together then? (634)

Obviously we need to admit that the American democratic myth is narrowly Euro-American, but such an admission is without value if it does not lead to a greater wisdom in discovering the complex inter-relationship of European, Indian, and African America. From the beginning the European's consciousness was affected by the Indian as much as the Indian's was affected by the European. And though some tribes have maintained much of their traditional culture, no tribal culture is what it was in 1492 or even a hundred years ago. First Europe and then European America have happened to Indian America for five hundred years because Europe and Indian America (and African America) have happened to all of us. As Stanley Crouch has said, "The American is an incontestable mix of blood, style, and tradition."

> Not for very long will we be able to accept the visions of the separatists ... because our history, public and private, has proven to us over and over that we were made for each other. [We] are too shot through with shared personal and historical resonances to separate. We are now and forever Americans, which means that we are in some very specific ways parts of all other peoples. Our culture and our bloodlines are cosmopolitan. No matter how hard we might try, we can't have it any other way (69).

Needless to say, our present cultural predicament suggests that such a view is hardly fashionable. Its polar opposite is that of Calvin Martin, who questions whether the American Indian can *ever* be integrated into "conventional" history. For Martin the historical vision of the European and the Indian are two mutually exclusive "thought worlds" (33), two "core philosophies" which he labels anthropological (European) and biological (Indian) (9), and the latter vision, being "mythic" (30), is so different, indeed so unique, in its view of time and space, so he claims, that European and Euro-American scholars may never understand it.

What are we to make of such an argument? Are we to assume that the "uniqueness" of Indians exempts them from the usual generalizations which we like to think can be made of all human beings everywhere? Is not the assumption of a universal humanity which transcends time and place and is to be seen in all peoples everywhere in history and culture the only thing that makes it possible for someone in our own century to understand the history of the Roman or Aztec empires or for a European to relate to the humanity of an African -- or vice versa? If it is really true that Indians perceive time and space in ways that non-Indians cannot -- which is another way of saying that Indians are unable to perceive time and space the way other people do -- then Indians are psychologically or physically or spiritually or somehow superior or inferior to non-Indians. If that isn't racism it certainly sounds like it. And if those who wish to deny that the Indian conception of time and space is not in the "blood" of Indians but is only cultural, then our answer must be that all human beings are at least potentially capable of something which enables them to put themselves into the minds of people unlike them in race -- imagination.

The truth is that any statement about the impact of the Indian on American culture must go beyond the usual elements that come to mind -- the influences on American speech, music, literature and art, to say nothing of clothing, games, agriculture, herbal medicine, and so on, moccasins and maize, *Tammany* and *caucus*. All of these are important but less important than the mysterious process by which, in the last five hundred years, Indians have become European, Europeans have become Indian, and both have become American, the process implied in Constance Rourke's remark that "the Backwoodsman conquered the Indian, but the Indian also conquered him" (40) and in the statement by Phillips D. Carleton, in his discussion of seventeenth and eighteenth century "captivity" literature, that "the Indian was the hammer that beat out a new race on the anvil of the continent" (180).

To attempt to understand this process we might consider one symbolic figure, one model for the way Indians adapted to the circumstances of the European invasion, and one example of the pitfalls that await the scholar who seeks to understand the Americanization of America.

Squanto, who encountered the Pilgrims at Plymouth in 1620, had been carried

to Spain as a slave by a passing English ship six years before. But he was freed
through the good offices of Spanish friars, reached England, where he was befriended
and employed by a London merchant, and eventually managed to return home, where
he found that European disease had killed off his people, the Patuxet band of
Wampanoags (Vaughan 16, 23). Bradford, the early governor of the Plymouth
colony, tells us that the Pilgrims were confounded by the appearance first of
Samoset, who had acquired broken English from fishermen in "the eastern parts"
(Maine), and then of Squanto, who served as their interpreter and taught them to use
fish as fertilizer in their fields of maize (110-112, 115-116). The image of Squanto
showing the Pilgrims how to put a small fish in every hill of corn is so venerable in
American legend that it surprises us to discover that there is no evidence that any
Indian tribe on the east coast of North America in 1620 used fish as fertilizer and that
no sixteenth or seventeenth century English, French or Dutch account of contact with
those tribes makes any mention of the practice. But fish *were* used for this purpose
in England at that time and in France from the Middle Ages on. Furthermore, the
practice was followed by those who manned England's fishing stations in
Newfoundland when Squanto, in an unsuccessful attempt to return to Massachusetts
Bay, was there for a year or two before he was able to return home in 1619. If he did
not see fish used as fertilizer in Europe he certainly must have seen the practice in
Newfoundland (Ceci 74-75) .

Squanto is therefore a figure of great symbolic significance: an
English-speaking, well-traveled Indian who taught Europeans how to raise an Indian
grain by what were almost certainly European methods. Our difficulty in separating
Indian and European elements in our history is present from the beginning, and
Squanto, as Lynn Ceci says, is a "culture-broker" (83), a term which might also be
applied to many, perhaps all, American Indian writers, whose work reveals the
complex interrelationship of tribal and "Euro-American" literary elements.

A model of the Indian's adaptation to the new circumstances created by the
European invasion is seen in James Axtell's explanation of why early English and,

in particular, French missionaries had such success in persuading Indians to convert to Christianity. Beyond the practical considerations -- political or military alliances, economic aid, trade advantages -- the individual Indian, Axtell says, was able simply to add Christian elements to his traditional religious notions by a syncretic process which insured that the latter could survive under the protective coloration of the religion of the invader (*After Columbus* 54, 117-118). Such a strategy ought to be remembered when we attempt to discover the truth about Black Elk's conversion to Roman Catholicism almost half a century before his death and his life-time allegiance to the terms of the great vision which he experienced at the age of nine -- as well as the use of that vision by John G. Neihardt in *Black Elk Speaks*. Was Black Elk's conversion and his Christian practice thereafter an act of social deception? Or did he resurrect an old Lakota faith for Neihardt's benefit? Or, as seems more likely, was he able to embrace Christianity because he saw in it essential similarities to Lakota religion and to his own great personal vision? Did he, in other words, succeed in maintaining his traditional faith because he embraced a new one? No matter how we answer these questions, they make clear the great complexity in the question of European and American Indian cultural relations.

The traps which await anyone who seeks to understand the inter-penetration of European and Indian elements in America are many. Their kind can be exemplified in the comparison which the Italian scholar Elemire Zolla makes of accounts of the Plains Indian sun dance in books by Chief Buffalo Child Long Lance and Luther Standing Bear. Zolla finds no "touch of supernatural life" in Standing Bear and condemns him for "demean[ing] himself as a white man might," whereas he believes that Long Lance's account, though it is second hand, "gives an impression of truthfulness ..." (246). But Zolla could not know Donald B. Smith's biography of Sylvester Clark Long, a North Carolina African American who called himself Long Lance, who sometimes has been identified parenthetically and with great historical vagueness as a "Croatan" -- today, presumably, he would be called a Lumbee -- and who may in fact have been part Indian, but certainly was not the Blackfoot he claimed to be. And if Standing Bear is not adequately "supernatural" to satisfy Zolla, he apparently was a Sioux Indian. If Zolla is right about the authenticity of the Indian supernaturalism of Long Lance, who was hardly an Indian at all, and the lack of it in Standing Bear, who was, then clearly the question of how Indian and non-Indian elements in American culture interrelate is complex.

The definition of the syncretic processes of American cultural history remains the greatest challenge to modern scholars in the study of the American past. I am convinced that when such a study is undertaken it will require recognition of two factors.

In the first place, the Indian is increasingly coming to be seen as the focus of spirituality in the American imagination, a spirituality associated in our culture with the American landscape, which is in a sense the physical manifestation of that spirituality. An illustration of how this has happened -- and of how the American consciousness is in part the result of the inter-penetration of Indian and European elements -- may be found in the idea of "Mother Earth," which, as Sam Gill has demonstrated, is found in the traditions of very few tribes, indeed almost none, but which began to emerge a century ago in the writings of white Americans, appeared in definitions of the American earth as an Indian queen or princess (5, 7, 153) -- the Pocahantas of Hart Crane's *The Bridge* may be the most obvious example -- and has been appropriated so universally by American Indians in this century that it is now easy to assume that it has always been a basic element in the mythology of every tribe. Given the commitment of Indians to the unique Indianness of the idea it is no wonder that their response to Gill's book was, to say the least, emphatic. (The fair reader of a hyperbolic example which is disgraced by conventional charges of "genocide" and even, by implication, Nazism -- Ward Churchill's "commentary" in *American Indian Culture and Research Journal*, 1988 -- will also read Gill's accompanying reply.) But in cultural and mythical terms the process by which Indians, in appropriating this idea, made it peculiarly Indian and returned it to the rest of our culture resembles the process by which Squanto learned from Europeans the use of fish fertilizer and then returned that knowledge, re-imagined as a basic element of American earth-lore, to Europeans who had not learned it in their own culture and, in the process of learning it in a new world, became to that extent American.

Another example of this process of inter-change of Indian and other elements in American culture may be seen in the "occupation" of Wounded Knee on the Pine Ridge Reservation in South Dakota in 1973 by AIM "activists." Why did they choose Wounded Knee? No doubt we must expect to be called cynics if we suggest that the entire enterprise had a lot to do with the workings of television, though the truth about it was clearly delineated at the time by a journalist named Terri Schultz in a revealing (and funny) article for which she wrote a splendid and suggestive title -- "Bamboozle Me Not at Wounded Knee." The truth is that the episode occurred in the aftermath of the publication of a best-seller by Dee Brown (*Bury My Heart at Wounded Knee*, 1970) and that the AIM leaders knew that because of public familiarity with Brown's title a clash at Wounded Knee would agitate the idealism of the greatest number of Americans. Surely this had more to do with their motives than any real concern for the plight of the Oglala Lakota of Pine Ridge. In other words, a white writer's work of history, including its account of the massacre of a band of Oglalas at Wounded Knee in 1890 -- or rather his title -- led to the choice of Wounded Knee for the "stand." But where did Brown get his title? Actually it is the last line of a poem by Stephen Vincent Benet called "American Names," written when Benet was in Paris writing *John Brown's Body* and expressing his homesickness in a catalogue of American place-names. For the sake of those names Benet rejects those of famous European places: "I shall not be there. I shall rise and pass. / Bury my heart at Wounded Knee." In fact, the poem has nothing at all to do with Indians. The process is like the swinging of a pendulum -- Indians naming a tiny creek in South Dakota, the name translated into English and becoming eventually the name of a village, a poet writing a poem which uses the village's name, among many others, as the ultimate expression of his sense of American identity, a historian writing a book about Indian-white conflict, including the terrible event at the village in 1890, and using the poet's language for purposes unintended in the poem, and Indian activists choosing the village as the scene for their heroics because the book was a best-seller.

This is a very American process -- and it reveals certain elements of exploitation. If it is true, as I am sure it is, that the Indian has come to embody spirituality in the American consciousness, then it also is true that the willingness to accept the Indian in these terms also can be exploited by non-Indians -- and Indians, too, for that matter -- if they think they have reasons for doing so. One wonders, for example, what motivated Ted Perry, creator of the bogus version of the famous speech made in 1854 by Chief Seattle (Sealth) during treaty negotiations with Governor Isaac Stevens, a piece of eloquence which, without editorial manipulation, belongs in the "canon" of our national literature. The core of what Seattle actually said is probably reflected in the 1887 text published by Dr. Henry Smith, who was there, may have known the Salish language or at least the Chinook trade language in which the negotiations, at least in part, probably were conducted, and made notes, which, unfortunately, have not survived. But in 1972 Perry, preparing a script for a film on behalf of environmental concerns, inserted "relevant" remarks into the speech, including Seattle's claim to have seen on the Great Plains the rotting remains of buffalo that had been shot from trains by white men -- in spite of the fact that neither Chief Seattle nor any railroad was present on the Plains in the mid-1850's. Perry's version of the speech soon was all over the place, in 1991 becoming the basis for a best-selling children's book called *Brother Eagle, Sister Sky: A Message from Chief Seattle*. Herman Viola, a Smithsonian scholar who ought to know better, has defended this case of what can only be called public lying: "There *was* some Indian out there who could have said that kind of thing." But Perry himself, twenty years after the first lie, has suggested that our willingness to embrace the bogus speech is further evidence of "placing Native Americans up on a pedestal and not taking responsibility for our own actions" (Jones).

But Perry is only partly right. To me it is obvious that the reception of his version of the speech, given its environmental thrust, must be due to a sense in the American public that the Indian, as the primary representative of our environmentalist concerns, is able to equate a superior spiritual awareness with the landscape itself.

At the same time, the physical and spiritual reality represented by the landscape and the Indian must be understood both in terms of the mind of Europe and the strong hearts and physical stamina of the African slaves whose presence in the American psyche is just as strong as the other elements and whose culture has affected our culture as a whole in innumerable ways. The descendants of those Africans have modified the consciousness of the entire American society and have been modified by it in becoming, in Albert Murray's useful term, "omni-Americans." Murray makes the point that "so-called" white and black Americans resemble no people in the world as much as they resemble each other: "American culture ... is patently and irrevocably composite [and] incontestably mulatto" (22).

This perception, as Murray acknowledges, derives from Constance Rourke's contention that our "national character" derives from three representative figures from our almost mythic past whom she characterizes in the first three chapters of *American Humor* -- the Yankee, the backwoodsman, and the Negro -- but the backwoodsman, as she makes clear, was in consciousness virtually an Indian and the Yankee was the American product of Europe. Her trio, in other words, is a variant of the pattern I have indicated -- European, Indian, African -- and the American landscape defines the variation. Rourke's Yankee, backwoodsman, and Negro are the European, the Indian, and the African *in the American landscape* once Englishmen settled Virginia and Massachusetts and the first Africans were landed at Jamestown. Every American, whether he or she knows it or not, is simultaneously a European *and* an African *and* an Indian living in the American landscape.

This is not to say, of course, that the sort of American of European descent who claims under the terms of our ideals of freedom that no one should have the right to tell him that he must stop polluting a river is particularly conscious of this. But then neither are those Indians in the Puget Sound country who, Duane Niatum tells us, have been caught killing endangered eagles for the substantial price they can get for their feathers (Bruchac, *Survival* 200). In our search for villains, in other words, we will find enough guilt to go around. We are not dealing here with such criminals but with ordinary, decent people who know, whatever else they know, that they are Americans and cannot be anything else.

A second factor to be remembered in research for a new comprehensive and syncretic American cultural history is that it might well reveal the characteristics of "metahistory." Most historians, assuming that poetry and history are two different things, employ the distinction made by Aristotle to the effect that history is limited to what actually happened while poetry tells us what, given the premises of the work, *ought* to happen, and they assume that whatever is "poetic" in a work of history compromises its historical value. But, as Northrop Frye has pointed out, the writer of "metahistory" finds the poetry in history, and in this respect "metahistory" takes on some of the quality of myth: " ... when a historian's scheme gets to a certain point of comprehensiveness it becomes mythical in shape" (53).

The thesis of Hayden White's study of nineteenth-century European historiography is that historical works "contain a deep structural content which is generally poetic, and specifically linguistic" and that this "deep structural content" is their "metahistorical" element (ix).

White has depended "heavily," he says (3n), on Northrop Frye's discussion, in *Anatomy of Criticism*, of patterns of symbolism in the four basic literary genres, and Frye, citing Gibbon, Spengler, and Toynbee as writers of "metahistorical" history, defines its four modes as romantic (the quest for the perfection of a classless society or the city of God), comic (progress through an evolutionary process), tragic (the decline and fall of nations), or ironic (recurrence and casual catastrophe). White's four representative nineteenth-century historians are Michelet (romance), von Ranke (comedy), de Tocqueville (tragedy), and Burckhardt (satire).

The fall of the Roman empire (Gibbon) and the decline of Western civilization (Spengler) are obvious subjects for the tragic mode, and we must assume that Toynbee, though Frye does not say so, wrote ironic "metahistory" and that Marx, to the extent that he was a historian, wrote in the romantic mode.

The comic mode is particularly significant in American historiography because of the example of George Bancroft. Deriving his moral ardor from his Puritan traditions and his political ideals from Jacksonian democracy, Bancroft narrated the development of ideals of American liberty from the original settling of America to the writing of the Constitution in the light of assumptions about a divine plan. Providence in his view assured appropriate conditions for the planting of free institutions in America and the achievement of democracy's "city upon a hill." For example, he assumed that Roman Catholicism deterred the development of democracy in Latin America and that freedom was possible in the United States because English colonization in North America was providentially delayed by the English Reformation.

And of course he had no difficulty justifying the providentially ordained conquest of the American earth, dismissing any Indian claim to it and indeed dismissing the landscape itself.

> Its only inhabitants were a few scattered tribes of feeble barbarians, destitute of commerce and of political connection. The axe and the ploughshare were unknown. The soil, which had been gathering fertility from the repose of centuries, was lavishing its strength in magnificent but useless vegetation (1: 3).

Certainly Bancroft's "metahistory" is "mythical in shape," and that shape is clearly related to what we have called the basic American myth of personal and economic freedom.

Indeed we must assume that Bancroft's history of the political origins of the United States contributed to the development of the democratic myth of America. We also must assume, therefore, that if the democratic myth has been essentially Euro-American and if the great task before all of us is to enhance the role of Indian elements in the myth, then the scholar who undertakes a comprehensive and indeed monumental study of the vast evidence of American cultural unity may make a significant contribution to the slow process of mythogenesis which we must hope will produce in time a yet untold myth which will unite a people who so far have remained divided by cultural differences.

Given my dismissal in the previous chapter of deconstructionist manipulations of the historical record for the sake of political ends and my willingness to admit that readers of that record too often believe only what they want to believe, some may wonder why I defend "metahistory," which may appear only another case of willfully imposing one's own dogma upon historical realities which may not support it. My answer to this is that my objection to history-writing as the zaniest proponents of desconstruction justify it is to their palming off political discourse as history. The great historians have worked in that field in which history and poetry overlap, and their best readers have not looked for justifications for their political prejudices but for the grandeur they have found in history as rendered in Shakespeare's history plays, which are more poetry than history, and in Gibbon's account of the disintegration of the Roman empire, which is more history than poetry. The historian who contributes to the world's body of literature will avoid not only the errors of the stylistic stumblebums who have produced too much of what has come out of universities but of those who paste up political billboards and call them history -- or literary criticism. Bancroft's history, after all, is still worth reading; it retains its poetry and thus its grandeur as a contribution to the creation of an American mythology which provided focus for those it united in their belief in American democracy in the nineteenth century. To recognize its incompleteness as history is not to be unmoved by its poetry.

In any case, present-day efforts to assert the claims of "multi-ethnicity" have done little to unite us. Indeed the strategy of these efforts seems implicitly to be derived from the assumption that a minority culture deserves attention only because it is utterly different from all others and that the irreconcilable opposition to each other of the several alleged American cultures must be maintained because there has never been and never should be an American "consensus." Presumably those who make this argument believe, without admitting or even recognizing the racist implications of what they are saying, that the only possible "consensus" would be so powerfully "Euro-American" that it would overwhelm the culture of any minority. They assume, in other words, that "minority" cultures require artificial walls for their defense because they are essentially weak.

But what is most wrong with dividing people by these artificial distinctions is that it depends upon our constantly keeping the bugaboo of race in the front of our minds. As Albert Murray says,

> [The United States] is a nation of multicolored people. [Any] fool can see that the white people are not really white, and that black people are not black. They are all interrelated in one way or another. ... [The] present domestic conflict and upheaval grows out of the fact that in spite of their common destiny and deeper interests, the people of the United States are being mislead by misinformation to insist on *exaggerating* their ethnic differences. The problem is not the existence of ethnic differences ... but the intrusion of such differences into areas where they do not belong (3).

And worse than that, this preoccupation with racial identity, even when it derives from good intentions, helps to perpetuate the racism it is meant to eliminate. This is precisely the point made by the sociologist Yehudi Webster: " ... it is neither race nor racism that bedevils American society, but that racial classification [which] enjoys a privileged status in social studies" (2). In defining problems according to race, Webster argues, both government and scholarship inevitably develop racial solutions which generate more problems (7).

> Racial solutions, such as busing, affirmative action, black power, and multiculturalism, are bound to fail, because they heighten the very racial awareness that is said to have led to 'racial problems' in the first place. Their failure is then conceived as proof that race is a hardened reality that has 'a life of its own.' ... Racially defined problems, by definition, cannot be resolved (21).

Of course, the monitoring of desegregation required the collection of data on the racial make-up of the population. But Webster argues that the use of racial classifications institutionalizes racial divisions, and those divisions then require "solutions" which create further racial awareness and thus further racial conflict.

To me it seems incontrovertible that virtually everything said about race is essentially nonsense and that emphasis on racial difference inevitably is at the expense of the claims of our common humanity. A more useful premise for our "multi-ethnic" concerns, I believe, is to be found in the abundant evidence that Indian and African and European elements in the American experience have been modifying each other from the beginning. The mutual impact of Indian America and European America and African America began almost at the first moment of contact and has continued at an accelerating pace to this day.

Because of the particular angle of vision which Indian writers share, our careful attention to what they write will illuminate the entire cultural history of our civilization. Simon Ortiz is right: "We are all with and within each other."

WORKS CITED

Adams, Alexander. *Geronimo*. Berkley Edition. New York: Berkley, 1972.

Allen, Paula Gunn, ed. *Spiderwoman's Granddaughters*. Boston: Beacon Press, 1989.

Axtell, James. "The Unkindest Cut, or Who Invented Scalping? A Case Study," in *The European and the Indian* (New York: Oxford University Press, 1981), pp. 16-35.

_____. *After Columbus*. New York: Oxford University Press, 1988.

_____. *Beyond 1492*. New York: Oxford University Press, 1992.

Bancroft, George. *The History of the United States of America from the Discovery of the Continent*, 6 vols. Centenary Edition. Boston: Little Brown, 1876-1879.

Beidler, Peter. *Fig Tree John: An Indian in Fact and Fiction*. Tucson: University of Arizona Press, 1977.

Berry, Brewton. *Almost White*. New York: Macmillan, 1963.

Bevis, William. "American Indian Verse Translations." *College English* 35 (March 1974): 693-703.

Blanche, Jerry D., ed. *Native American Reader: Stories, Speeches, and Poems*. Juneau, AK: Denali Press, 1990.

Blu, Karen I. *The Lumbee Problem. The Making of an American Indian People*. Cambridge, UK: Cambridge University Press, 1980.

Boas, Franz. "The Methods of Ethnology." *American Anthropologist* n.s. 22 (October-December 1920): 311-321.

Bourne, Randolph S. "Trans-National America." *Atlantic Monthly* 118 (July 1916): 86-97.

Bradford's History of Plymouth Plantation, ed. William T. Davis. New York: Scribner's, 1908.

Brandon, William. *New World for Old*: *Reports from the New World and their Effects on the Development of Social Thought in Europe, 1500-1800*. Athens, OH: Ohio University Press, 1986.

Bruchac, Joseph. *Survival This Way. Interviews with American Indian Poets*. Tucson: University of Arizona Press, 1987.

_____, ed. *New Voices from the Longhouse*: *An Anthology of Contemporary Iroquois Writing*. Greenfield Center, NY: Greenfield Review Press, 1989.

_____, ed. *Raven Tells Stories*: *An Anthology of Alaskan Native Writing*. Greenfield Center, NY: Greenfield Review Press, 1991.

Carleton, Phillips D. "The Indian Captivity." *American Literature* 15 (May 1943): 169-180.

Ceci, Lynn. "Squanto and the Pilgrims: On Planting Corn 'in the Manner of the Indians,'" in Clifton, *The Invented Indian*, pp. 71-89.

Churchill, Ward. "Sam Gill's Mother Earth: Colonialism, Genocide and the Expropriation of Indigenous Spiritual Tradition in Contemporary Academia." *American Indian Culture and Research Journal* 12:3 (1988): 49-68.

Clements, William M. "Faking the Pumpkin: On Jerome Rothenberg's Literary Offenses." *Western American Literature* 16 (Fall 1981): 193-204.

Clifton, James A. "Alternate Identities and Cultural Frontiers," in *Being and Becoming Indian*, ed. James A. Clifton (Chicago: Dorsey Press, 1989), pp. 1-37.

_____, ed. *The Invented Indian. Cultural Fictions and Government Policies*. New Brunswick, NJ: Transaction Publishers, 1990.

Coltelli, Laura. *Winged Words*: *American Indian Writers Speak*. Lincoln: University of Nebraska Press, 1990.

Cook-Lynn, Elizabeth. "American Indian Intellectualism and the New Indian Story." *American Indian Quarterly* 20 (Winter 1996): 57-76.

Corle, Edwin. *Fig Tree John*. New York: Liveright, 1971.

Costo, Rupert, and Jeannette Henry. *Textbooks and the American Indian.* San Francisco: The Indian Historian Press, 1970.

Costo, Rupert, and Jeannette Henry, eds. *The Missions of California: A Legacy of Genocide.* San Francisco: Indian Historian Press, 1987.

Countryman, Edward. *Americans. A Collision of Histories.* New York: Hill and Wang, 1996.

Crouch, Stanley. "The One-Out-of-Many Blues," in Royal, pp. 63-69.

Daniels, John. "The Indian Population of North America in 1492." *William and Mary Quarterly,* 3rd Series 49 (April 1992): 298-320.

Dauenhauer, Nora Marks, and Richard Dauenhauer, eds. *Haa Shuka, Our Ancestors: Tlingit Oral Narratives.* Seattle: University of Washington Press, 1987.

_____. *Haa Tuwunaagu Yis, for Healing Our Spirits: Tlingit Oratory.* Seattle: University of Washington Press, 1991.

Deloria, Vine, Jr. "Comfortable Fictions and the Struggle for Turf: An Essay Review of *The Invented Indian: Cultural Fictions and Governmental Policies.*" *American Indian Quarterly* 16 (Summer 1992): 397-410.

DeMallie, Raymond J., ed. *The Sixth Grandfather.* Lincoln: University of Nebraska Press, 1984.

Feraca, Stephen E. *Why Don't They Give Them Guns? The Great American Indian Myth.* Lanham, MD: University Press of America, 1990.

Frye, Northrop. *Fables of Identity. Studies in Poetic Mythology.* New York: Harcourt, Brace and Jovanovich, 1963.

Gill, Sam. *Mother Earth. An American Story.* Chicago: University of Chicago Press, 1987.

_____. "The Power of Story." *American Indian Culture and Research Journal* 12:3 (1988): 69-84.

Grinde, Donald A. "The Iroquois and the Nature of American Government." *American Indian Culture and Research Journal* 17 (1993): 153-173.

Hagan, William T. "Full Blood, Mixed Blood, Generic, and Ersatz. The Problem of Indian Identity." *Arizona and the West* (1986): 309-326.

Healy, George R. "The French Jesuits and the Idea of a Noble Savage." *William and Mary Quarterly*, Series III, 15 (April 1958): 143-167.

Henige, David. "Their Numbers Become Thick: Native American Historical Demography as Expitation," in Clifton, *The Invented Indian*, pp. 169-191.

Henson, Lance. *Selected Poems 1970-1983*. Greenfield Center, NY: Greenfield Review Press, 1985.

_____. *Another Distance: New and Selected Poems*. Norman, OK: Point Riders, 1991.

_____. *Poems for a master beadworker / Gedichte für eine meisterin im perlensticken*. Osnabruck, Germany: OBEMA, 1993.

Hinton, Leanne, and Lucille J. Watahomigie, eds. *Spirit Mountain: An Anthology of Yuman Story and Song*. Tucson: University of Arizona Press, 1984.

Hobson, Geary, ed. *The Remembered Earth. An Anthology of Contemporary Native American Literature*. Albuquerque, NM: Red Earth Press, 1979.

_____. "The Rise of the White Shaman as a New Version of Cultural Imperialism," in *The Remembered Earth*, pp. 100-108.

_____. "The Literature of Indian Oklahoma." *World Literature Today* 64 (Summer 1990): 426-430.

Johansen, Bruce E. *Forgotten Founders. How the American Indian Helped Shape Democracy*. Boston: Harvard Common Press, 1982.

Jones, Malcolm, Jr. "Just Too Good to be True." *Newsweek*, May 4, 1992, p. 68.

Kehoe, Alice B. "Primal Gaia: Primitivists and Plastic Medicine Men," in Clifton, pp. 193-209.

Kenny, Maurice. *Between Two Rivers. Selected Poems 1956-1984*. Fredonia, NY: White Pine Press, 1987.

_____. *Tekonwatonti / Molly Brant*. Fredonia, NY: White Pine Press, 1992.

King, Thomas. *Green Grass, Running Water*. Boston: Houghton Mifflin, 1993.

Krupat, Arnold. *The Voice in the Margin. Native American Literatures and the Canon*. Berkeley: University of California Press, 1989.

Larson, Charles R. *American Indian Fiction*. Albuquerque: University of New Mexico Press, 1978.

Lawrence, D.H. *Studies in Classic American Literature*. New York: Seltzer, 1923.

Lerner, Andrea, ed. *Dancing on the Rim of the World: An Anthology of Contemporary Northwest Native American Writing*. Tucson: University of Arizona Press, 1990.

Littlefield, Daniel F., Jr. "American Indians, American Scholars and the American Literary Canon." *American Studies* (University of Kansas) 33:2 (1992): 95-111.

MacLeod, William Christie. *The American Indian Frontier*. New York: Alfred Knopf, 1928.

Martin, Calvin, ed. *The American Indian and the Problem of History*. New York: Oxford University Press, 1987.

Mayer, Allan J. "Is This Tribe Indian?" *Newsweek*, January 7, 1980, p. 32.

McAllister, H.S. "'The Language of Shamans': Jerome Rothenberg's Contribution to American Indian Literature." *Western American Literature* 10 (February 1976): 293-309).

McNichols, Charles L. *Crazy Weather*. New York: Macmillan, 1944.

_____. "The Buck in the Bush." *Harper's* 189 (July 1944): 126-128.

Means, Russell, with Marvin J. Wolf. *Where White Men Fear to Tread*. New York: St. Martin's, 1995.

Miller, Walter James. "Edwin Corle and the American Dilemma," in Corle, pp. ix-xviii.

Momaday, N. Scott. *House Made of Dawn*. New York: Harper and Row, 1968.

146

_____. *The Way to Rainy Mountain*. Albuquerque: University of New Mexico Press, 1969.

Murray, Albert. *The Omni Americans*. New York: Da Capo Press, n.d. (Original publication: 1970.)

Neihardt, John G. *Black Elk Speaks*. Lincoln: University of Nebraska Press, 1961.

Niatum, Duane, ed. *Harper's Anthology of 20th Century Native American Poetry*. Harper San Francisco, 1988.

Ortiz, Simon. *From Sand Creek*. Oak Park, NY: Thunder's Mouth Press, 1981.

Owens, Louis. *Other Destinies. Understanding the American Indian Novel*. Norman: University of Oklahoma Press, 1992.

Powers, William K. *Oglala Religion*. Lincoln: University of Nebraska Press, 1977.

Rothenberg, Jerome, ed. *Shaking the Pumpkin*: *Traditional Poetry of the Indian North Americans*. Rev. ed. New York: Van der Marck, 1986.

Rothenberg, Jerome, and Diane Rothenberg, eds. *Symposium of the Whole*: *A Range of Discourse toward an Ethnopoetics*. Berkeley: University of California Press, 1983.

Rourke, Constance. *American Humor*. New York: Harcourt, Brace, 1931.

Royal, Robert, ed. *Reinventing the American People*. Washington: Ethics and Public Policy Center, 1995.

Sanders, Thomas E. "Tribal Literature: Individual Identity and the Collective Unconscious." *College Composition and Communication* 24 (October 1973): 256-266.

Schlesinger, Arthur. "A Dissent on Multicultural Education." *Partisan Review* 58 (1991): 630-634.

Schultz, Terri. "Bamboozle Me Not at Wounded Knee." *Harper's*, June 1973, pp. 46-56.

Shalit, Wendy. "A Ladies' Room of One's Own." *Commentary*, August 1995, pp. 33-37.

Silko, Leslie Marmon. *Ceremony*. Penguin Edition. New York: Viking Penguin, 1986.

_____. "An Old-Time Indian Attack Conducted in Two Parts," in Hobson, *The Remembered Earth*, pp. 195-200.

Simard, Jean-Jacques. "White Ghosts, Red Shadows: The Reduction of North American Natives," in Clifton, *The Invented Indian*, pp. 333-369.

Smith, Donald B. *Long Lance. The True Story of an Impostor*. Lincoln: University of Nebraska Press, 1982.

Stannard, David E. *American Holocaust. Columbus and the Conquest of the New World*. New York: Oxford University Press, 1992.

Statistical Abstract of the United States 1994. U.S. Bureau of the Census. Washington, D.C., 1994.

Swann, Brian, and Arnold Krupat, eds. *I Tell You Now: Autobiographical Essays by Native American Writers*. Lincoln: University of Nebraska Press, 1987.

Todorov, Tzvetlan. *The Conquest of America*. New York: Harper and Row, 1982.

Tooker, Elisabeth. "The United States Constitution and the Iroquois League." *Ethnohistory* 35 (Fall 1988): 305-336.

Vaughan, Alden T. *New England Frontier. Puritans and Indians 1620-1675*. Boston: Little, Brown, 1965.

_____. "From White Man to Redskin: Changing Anglo-American Perceptions of the American Indian." *American Historical Review* 87 (October 1982): 917-953.

Vizenor, Gerald. *The Everlasting Sky. New Voices from the People Named the Chippewa*. New York: Crowell-Collier Press, 1972.

_____. *Landfill Meditation*. Middletown, CT: Wesleyan University Press, 1991.

_____. *Manifest Manners: Postindian Warriors of Survivance*. Hanover, NH: University Press of New England, 1994.

Webster, Yehudi O. *The Racialization of America*. New York: St. Martin's, 1992.

148

Welch, James. *Winter in the Blood.* Penguin Edition. New York: Viking Penguin, 1986.

White, Hayden. *Metahistory. The Historical Imagination in Nineteenth-Century Europe.* Baltimore: Johns Hopkins University Press, 1973.

White, Richard. "The Winning of the West: The Expansion of the Western Sioux in the Eighteenth and Nineteenth Centuries." *Journal of American History* 65 (September 1978): 319-343.

Young, Philip. "The Mother of Us All: Pocohantas Reconsidered," in *Three Bags Full. Essays in American Fiction* (New York: Harcourt Brace Jovanovich, 1972), pp.175-203.

Zolla, Elemire. *The Writer and the Shaman. A Morphology of the American Indian.* Trans. Raymond Rosenthal. New York: Harcourt, Brace and Jovanovich, 1969.

Zuni: Selected Writings of Frank Hamilton Cushing, ed. Jesse Green. Lincoln: University of Nebraska Press, 1979.

INDEX

NATIVE AMERICAN STUDIES